Tastes Like SCHITT

THE UNOFFICIAL *SCHITT'S CREEK* *Cookbook*

DELICIOUS RECIPES **75** INSPIRED BY THE SHOW

RACHEL & HANNAH FLOYD

THIS COOKBOOK WAS born much like baby Roland Moira Schitt was—surprisingly and under strange circumstances. During the height of a global pandemic, amidst a Netflix series about captive big cats and everyone and their mother developing their respective sourdough-baking skills, my sister and I joked about ways to stay sane during a time that felt, well, I won't say the word. We joked about writing a cookbook based on *Schitt's Creek*, a show that was responsible for a lot of joy and lightness during an otherwise dim time. We joked, and revisited, and joked and revisited and ultimately decided that in the midst of an uncertain future, there was, in fact, no time quite like the present. We compiled recipe after recipe, giggling to each other over hours of FaceTime calls across state lines. The project was a bridge during the longest time we'd gone without seeing each other in person.

We're delighted to have been able to create a revised and expanded edition of our original book, complete with our favorite bits of trivia about the show and gorgeous photos that feature the dishes we hope will soon become your favorites. All of these meals and drinks are based on your favorite *Schitt's Creek* characters, episodes, and fleeting moments, and we hope that as you work your way through them you'll find as much laughter and lightness as we did while creating them. Be sure to try the Farm Witches Peanut Butter Things; they're our personal favorite and definitely worth circling back for. Without further ado, our bébé, *Tastes Like Schitt*.

TABLE OF CONTENTS:

BREAKFASTS

TO START ANY PEREGRINATION ON A HIGH NOTE, ONLY THE MOST SCRUMPTIOUS REPAST WILL DO.

Unwanted Scones, pg. 20

RAY'S BUTTERMILK PANCAKES

Knock, knock! It's pancakes!
Stop your snuggle sesh and grab the maple syrup.

INGREDIENTS

- 1 cup all-purpose flour
- 2 Tbsp white sugar
- 1 tsp baking powder
- ½ tsp baking soda
- ½ tsp salt
- 1 egg
- 2 Tbsp melted butter
- 1 cup buttermilk
- Cooking spray

DIRECTIONS

1. Combine flour, sugar, baking powder, baking soda, and salt in a medium bowl.

2. Whisk together egg, melted butter, and buttermilk in a large bowl.

3. Add the dry mixture into the wet ingredients and whisk again, stopping as soon as the lumps are gone.

4. Heat a skillet over medium and coat with cooking spray.

5. Pour ¼ cup batter into the skillet. Cook until bubbles appear on the surface and the surface appears dry, about 2 to 3 minutes. Flip with a spatula, then cook until lightly browned on the other side, about 2 minutes.

6. Serve with syrup, butter, or jam.

**MAKES 6–8 PANCAKES OR
ENOUGH FOR A HUNGRY DAVID**

TRIVIA

Some of Ray's jobs throughout the series include: real estate agent, photographer, home organizer, and Christmas tree salesman.

NO ROOM SERVICE BERRY PARFAIT

There is no room service at the Rosebud Motel,
but there is a cafe across the street.

INGREDIENTS

- ⅓ cup blackberries
- 6 oz vanilla Greek yogurt
- ½ banana, sliced
- ⅓ cup granola
- ⅓ cup sliced strawberries
- ⅓ cup blueberries

DIRECTIONS

1. In a tall parfait glass, layer the blackberries, a heaping spoonful of yogurt, one-third of the banana slices, and about 2 Tbsp of granola.
2. Repeat the layers with strawberries and blueberries until all of the ingredients have been used.
3. Place the parfait on a tray with a tall spoon, a napkin, and a single bloom in a tasteful bud vase. Set the tray outside your door and close it. Pretend to hear a knock on your door. Open it and voilà! Perhaps the motel does have room service after all!

MAKES 1 PARFAIT

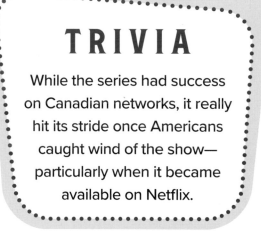

TRIVIA

While the series had success on Canadian networks, it really hit its stride once Americans caught wind of the show—particularly when it became available on Netflix.

BOB'S BAGELS

Good bagels—the real way. Schitt's Creek never got the bagel shop it deserved, but these are simple to make at home.

INGREDIENTS

BAGELS

1⅛	tsp active dry yeast
2¼	cups warm water
3	Tbsp sugar, divided
1	Tbsp vegetable oil
7	cups bread flour, divided
1	Tbsp salt

TOPPINGS, AS DESIRED

3	Tbsp poppy seeds
3	Tbsp sea salt
3	Tbsp minced dried onion

DIRECTIONS

1. In a large bowl, add the yeast to warm water and stir gently to dissolve. Add 2 Tbsp of sugar, oil, 6 cups flour, and salt. Mix thoroughly until the dough comes together and separates from the sides of the bowl.

2. Coat a work surface with flour. Dump the dough onto the floured surface and knead, adding additional flour as necessary. Bagel dough should be fairly stiff. Work in as much extra flour as you can knead with ease. If using a stand mixer with a dough hook attachment, knead until the dough is smooth and elastic, about 8 minutes. If kneading by hand, knead for 12 to 15 minutes.

3. Roll the dough into a ball, then set it in a large, oiled bowl and turn to coat. Cover with a kitchen towel and let the dough rise until doubled in size, about 1 hour.

4. Punch down the dough and divide it into three equal pieces. Divide each of those pieces into four equal pieces and roll each one into a ball. You should have 12 evenly sized dough balls.

5. Take a ball in your hands and poke a hole in the middle using your thumbs. With your thumbs in the center, stretch outward, enlarging the hole and using your hands to make a bagel shape.

6. Repeat process with the remaining balls.

7. Place the bagels on two nonstick baking pans. Cover and let rest for 20 minutes.

8. Pour each topping on a plate and set aside.

9. While the bagels are resting, fill a large saucepan two-thirds full with water. Add the remaining 1 Tbsp sugar and bring to a boil. Drop a few bagels into the water at a time, being careful not to crowd. They should rise to the surface. Cook for 30 seconds on each side.

10. After removing each bagel from the water, drain it briefly, then dip the top of the bagel onto the topping plates. Evenly space bagels on two nonstick baking pans or very lightly oiled baking sheets.

11. Preheat the oven to 500 degrees F. Place

the bagels in the oven, and using a spray bottle filled with water, spray the inside of the oven 5 to 10 times, then quickly shut the door. This will create the steam that gives your bagels their light and chewy texture.

12. Bake for 2 minutes before reducing the temperature to 425 degrees F. Bake until well-browned, about 20 minutes.

MAKES 12 BAGELS

HANGOVER HOLLANDAISE

While this is good enough to eat at room temperature
out of a bowl, it is best when served over a classic eggs Benedict
and sprinkled with more cayenne.

INGREDIENTS

4 egg yolks
1 Tbsp freshly squeezed lemon juice
½ cup unsalted butter, melted
Pinch of cayenne pepper
Pinch of salt

DIRECTIONS

1. Fill a medium pot over high heat with 1 to 2 inches of water. Bring to a simmer, then lower the heat to medium-low to keep the water at a simmer.

2. Add the yolks and lemon juice to a metal bowl. Whisk the liquid until the mixture is thick and has doubled in volume. Place the bowl over the pot with barely simmering water, making sure that the water doesn't touch the bottom of the bowl. Continue to whisk quickly. Don't let the eggs get too hot or they will scramble.

3. Pour in the melted butter slowly and continue to whisk until the sauce has thickened and increased in volume.

4. Remove the bowl from the heat and whisk in the cayenne and salt. Serve immediately while hot or let it sit on the counter if you have a Johnny Rose-style hangover.

MAKES 1 CUP

TIPS AND TRICKS

Hollandaise is one of the five mother sauces, along with Béchamel, Espagnole, Sauce Tomate (Tomato), and Velouté. Learn to make them all!

MOIRA'S FRUIT CUP

A Café Tropical favorite, located on page 8 of the menu.
Goes well with a cup of tea.

INGREDIENTS

DRESSING

  1 heaping Tbsp honey

     Zest of 1 lemon

  1 Tbsp lemon juice

  1 Tbsp warm water

¼ tsp cinnamon

     Pinch of sea salt

FRUIT CUP

  1 cup pomegranate arils

  1 pear, diced

  2 medium apples, diced (Honeycrisp or similar)

1½ cups grapes, halved

DIRECTIONS

1. In a small bowl, combine the dressing ingredients. Set aside.

2. In a large bowl, combine the fruit. Add the dressing and toss gently to combine.

3. Place in the fridge for at least 30 minutes before serving to allow the flavors to meld.

MAKES 4 SERVINGS

TIPS AND TRICKS

The options for customizing this fruit cup are as plentiful as Moira's wig collection. Stick to fruits that are in season to freshen up your fruit cup.

CHEESEMAKER QUICHE

This quiche is vivacious, and that is not a word
we use to describe quiche often, but this flavorful combination
of goat cheese and onion is hard to beat.

INGREDIENTS

- 1 Tbsp olive oil
- 1 small yellow onion, diced
- 3 eggs
- ½ cup heavy cream
- ½ cup milk
- ½ tsp dried basil
- ½ tsp dried oregano
- 1 tsp kosher salt
- ½ tsp ground black pepper
- 1 (9-inch) pie crust
- 6 oz fresh chèvre
- 3 oz cheddar cheese, shredded

DIRECTIONS

1. Preheat the oven to 375 degrees F.

2. Heat the oil in a skillet over medium heat. Add onion and saute until soft and translucent, about 3 to 5 minutes.

3. In a medium bowl, whisk eggs, cream, milk, basil, oregano, salt, and pepper.

4. Prepare your pie crust by pressing the dough into a 9-inch pie pan. If you are using a store-bought pie crust, follow the package instructions.

5. Add the sauteed onions into the unbaked pie crust. Using a rubber spatula, distribute the onions evenly. Pour in the egg mixture.

6. Crumble the chèvre evenly over the egg mixture in pebble-sized chunks.

7. Sprinkle the cheddar on top.

8. Bake until a toothpick inserted into the center of the quiche comes out clean, about 22 to 30 minutes. The top should be browned and bubbly.

MAKES 6–8 SERVINGS

TRIVIA

Very few lines in the show were improvised. While a few jokes were written last minute, some were added during the table reads.

ROSEBUD CINNAMON ROLLS

The perfect cinnamon rolls to enjoy with some vodka, they're festive in a Scandinavian sort of way. These buns are made in muffin cups, so they're perfect for sharing, just not with Frank, since he didn't bring any quarry rocks.

INGREDIENTS

CINNAMON ROLLS

- ¾ cup milk
- ¼ cup butter, softened
- 3½–3¾ cups all-purpose flour, divided
- 1 (.25-oz) package instant yeast
- ¼ cup sugar
- ½ tsp salt
- ¼ cup water
- 1 egg

FILLING

- 1 cup brown sugar, packed
- 1 Tbsp ground cinnamon
- ½ cup butter, softened

DIRECTIONS

1. Warm the milk in a small saucepan just until it bubbles, then remove from heat. Mix in the butter and stir until melted. Cool this mixture until lukewarm.

2. In a large mixing bowl, combine 2¼ cups flour, yeast, sugar, and salt and mix well. Add the water, egg, and milk mixture and beat well. Add the remaining flour, a half cup at a time, stirring well after each addition. When the dough has just pulled together, turn it out onto a lightly floured surface and knead until smooth, about 5 minutes.

3. Cover the dough with a damp kitchen towel and let it rest 10 minutes.

4. Mix together the filling ingredients in a small bowl.

5. Roll out the dough into a 14-by-9-inch rectangle. Cover the surface of the dough with the filling.

6. Roll up the dough tightly into a log and pinch the seam to seal. Cut the log into 16 equal-size rolls and place the rolls cut side up into the lightly greased muffin cups. You will need to bake two batches. Cover and let them rise until doubled in size, about 30 minutes.

7. While the dough is proving, preheat the oven to 375 degrees F.

8. Bake the cinnamon rolls for 15 to 18 minutes or until browned. Remove from the muffin cups to cool. Top with either the cream cheese icing or the browned butter and apple cider glaze.

CREAM CHEESE ICING, OPTIONAL

- 1 (8-oz) package cream cheese, softened
- ½ cup butter, softened
- 1 tsp vanilla extract
- 3 cups confectioner's sugar
- 1 Tbsp milk

In a large bowl, combine all ingredients, beat until creamy and spread over the buns.

BROWNED BUTTER AND APPLE CIDER GLAZE, OPTIONAL

- 2 cups apple cider
- 4 Tbsp unsalted butter
- 2½ cups confectioner's sugar
  Pinch of salt

1. In a medium saucepan, heat apple cider over medium heat. Simmer until it has reduced to half cup of liquid.

2. Meanwhile, heat butter in a skillet over low-medium heat until it is lightly browned and smells nutty. Mix the butter into the apple cider.

3. Add in the confectioner's sugar and salt and mix until combined. If it is too thin, add additional confectioner's sugar. Pour over the buns.

MAKES 16 ROLLS

UNWANTED SCONES

Dear, there's nothing wrong with treating yourself, and these luscious scones are definitely a treat. The secret is in the way the butter is incorporated, which results in buttery, moist scones every time.

INGREDIENTS

SCONES

- 1 cup heavy cream, plus extra for brushing
- 8 Tbsp butter
- 2 cups all-purpose flour
- 1 Tbsp baking powder
- ¼ cup sugar
- ½ tsp salt
- ½ cup dried tart cherries
- ½ cup chopped pecans
- Zest of 1 orange

ORANGE-VANILLA GLAZE

- 1 Tbsp orange juice
- 2–3 Tbsp heavy cream
- 2 Tbsp butter
- 2 Tbsp dark brown sugar, sifted
- 1 tsp vanilla extract
- 1½ cups powdered sugar, sifted

DIRECTIONS

1. Preheat the oven to 400 degrees F. Line a baking sheet with parchment paper.

2. Place 1 cup heavy cream in the freezer to chill for at least 10 minutes.

3. Place butter in a microwave-safe mug and heat for 40 seconds or until melted. Set aside to cool.

4. In a large mixing bowl, whisk flour, baking powder, sugar, salt, cherries, and pecans.

5. Mix the orange zest into the chilled heavy cream with a fork. Slowly pour in the melted butter while stirring quickly with a fork. The butter should form tiny clumps.

6. Add the butter/cream mixture to the dry ingredients and stir with a rubber spatula until the flour is incorporated and a dough is just formed. Don't overmix.

7. Place the dough onto a work surface with flour and lightly dust with flour. Knead the dough six to seven times, then form into a disc measuring approximately 7 inches in diameter. Cut the dough into 8 equal wedges and transfer onto the baking sheet. Brush the tops with heavy cream. Bake for 15 to 17 minutes or until lightly browned.

8. Meanwhile, place orange juice, heavy cream, butter and brown sugar in a medium-size microwave-safe bowl. Microwave the mixture for 1 minute, then whisk well to smooth out any lumps.

9. Quickly whisk in the vanilla extract and powdered sugar to give the glaze the texture of honey. If the glaze is too thin, add more powdered sugar; if it is too thick, add more heavy cream.

10. Pour the glaze into a piping bag or quart-sized plastic storage bag (for the latter, cut off the tip). Drizzle the glaze over the scones before serving.

MAKES 8 SCONES

HELPFUL HALF MUFFINS

Will these blueberry muffins be helpful when you're considering uprooting your entire life to move to an apartment that was in season 3 of *Sex and the City*? Well, no. But are they delicious enough to distract you for a minute? Only if you eat one whole.

INGREDIENTS

- 1 cup oat milk
- 1 tsp apple cider vinegar
- 2 cups all-purpose flour
- 2½ tsp baking powder
- ¼ tsp baking soda
- ½ tsp salt
- ½ cup plus 2 Tbsp sugar
- ¼ cup plus 2 Tbsp canola oil
- 1 tsp vanilla extract
- Zest of 1 lemon
- 1½–2 cups frozen blueberries

DIRECTIONS

1. Preheat the oven to 375 degrees F.

2. Spray a muffin tin with cooking spray and set aside. In a small bowl, combine the oat milk and apple cider vinegar. Set aside to allow milk to curdle.

3. In a large bowl, combine the flour, baking powder, baking soda, and salt. Set aside. In a medium bowl, mix together the sugar, canola oil, vanilla extract, and lemon zest. Add the oat milk mixture and stir to combine. Stir in the dry ingredients until just incorporated—do not overmix. Fold in the blueberries.

4. Spoon the batter into muffin tins, filling each cup about ¾ full. Bake for 25 to 30 minutes until a toothpick inserted in the middle comes out clean.

5. Allow muffins to cool before removing from the pan. Eat half and offer the other half to your business partner/boyfriend.

MAKES 12 MUFFINS

TRIVIA

Dan Levy said he was nervous about filming the lip sync scene in season 4, episode 9. Before filming, he and Noah Reid split a bottle of Prosecco over lunch to loosen him up.

MOTEL COOKING

IF YOU EVER FIND YOURSELF trapped in a motel and the cafe nearest to you has already closed for the night, don't fret! Using only a coffeepot, microwave, a clothing iron, and a few other supplies, a prestidigitator like you will have no trouble whipping up a feast.

While these recipes aren't much to write home about, they may help to feed you in a pinch when you don't have access to a full kitchen. Read on to discover how easy it is to tap into your culinary creativity and make even the most run-down roadside motel room feel like home.

"BAKED" POTATOES

SUPPLIES a microwave, a plate or bowl, a metal fork

INGREDIENTS 1–2 medium potatoes, salt

Optional butter, salsa, sour cream, shredded cheese, bacon bits

DIRECTIONS

1. Use a metal fork to pierce each potato several times.

2. Microwave the potatoes on a plate for 3 to 4 minutes on high. Flip the potatoes and microwave for an additional 3 to 4 minutes. Check for doneness using the fork. The potato should pierce easily all the way through, but if not, cook in 1-minute increments. Once the potato is done, cut it down the center and add salt and any additional toppings.

Makes 1–2 servings

COFFEE POT EGGS

SUPPLIES a standard coffee maker, a bucket of ice

INGREDIENTS eggs, salt

Optional salsa, sour cream, precooked chicken

DIRECTIONS

1. Fill up the coffee carafe with water as though you were going to brew three-quarters of a pot of coffee.

2. Add the water to the reservoir, but instead of adding coffee grounds, take 3 to 4 eggs and gently set them in the empty coffee carafe.

3. Place the carafe back on the burner and turn the coffee pot on to start "brewing." The coffee pot will heat the water, which will eventually cover the eggs. It will take much longer than traditional hard-boiled eggs as the water temperature is much lower. The eggs will firm up as they slowly cook, but will be more similar to a soft-boiled egg.

4. After 40 to 45 minutes, carefully remove an egg to check its doneness. If the texture is acceptable, remove the carafe, gently pour out the water, and place the remaining eggs on ice to stop the cooking. If the test egg is not done, let the others continue to cook for 10 to 15 more minutes. Depending on the size and type of coffee pot, the cooking time will vary. It is good to start with more eggs than you need so you can test them for doneness. Once you get the hang of it, you'll be making breakfast in no time. Use this technique to cook an egg for Coffee Pot Ramen.

Makes 2 eggs

COFFEE POT RAMEN

SUPPLIES a clean coffee pot, a bowl, a fork or chopsticks

INGREDIENTS a packet of instant ramen

Optional Coffee Pot Eggs, precooked chicken, hot sauce, soy sauce

DIRECTIONS

1. Fill the carafe with water as though you were going to brew half a pot of coffee. Add water to the reservoir.

2. Place the carafe back on the burner and turn the coffee pot on to start "brewing."

3. Once the water has gone through, take the carafe off the burner and add ramen, breaking it up only enough to make it fit. Do not add the seasoning packet. Let the noodles cook for 15 to 20 minutes, then check for doneness. If the texture is soft enough, gently pour out some of the water. Pour the remaining noodles and some cooking water into a bowl and add the flavor packet. The more water you retain, the more diluted the seasoning packet will be. Add any additional toppings if using.

Makes 1 serving

MOTEL MOCHA

SUPPLIES a coffee cup, something to stir with

INGREDIENTS a packet of hot chocolate mix, coffee

DIRECTIONS

Follow the directions on the hot chocolate pouch but substitute hot coffee for hot water. Stir thoroughly and enjoy!

Makes 1 serving

QUESADILLA

SUPPLIES a clothing iron, an ironing board, tinfoil

INGREDIENTS small corn or flour tortillas, shredded cheese

Optional salsa, sour cream, precooked chicken

DIRECTIONS

1. Heat your iron on medium.

2. While it heats up, cut a piece of tinfoil that is a few inches wider than your tortilla. Place the tortilla in the center of the foil and add a thin layer of shredded cheese to half of it. If using, add a few pieces of chicken and fold the tortilla over itself. Next, fold the tinfoil over the folded tortilla so that it is covered entirely. Fold the open edges to create an envelope. This will ensure the cheese doesn't melt out and get stuck to the iron.

3. Cook the tortilla by setting the iron directly on it, so that the entire surface of the tortilla is underneath the iron. Do not press down as if you are pressing clothes, as this will squish out the cheese. Leave the iron on for 3 to 4 minutes and then flip the foil pouch over. Cook the other side for 2 to 3 minutes until the cheese is fully melted. Remove from the foil pouch and enjoy with whatever toppings you may have on hand.

Makes 1 quesadilla

Goat Cheese Nom Noms,
pg. 34

APPETIZERS

GOURMANDS TAKE NOTE: THESE SUMPTUOUS STARTERS WILL TURN A KATZENJAMMER OF A DAY INTO A JOCUND JAMBOREE.

BEDEVILED EGGS

These spicy hors d'oeuvres are perfect for when you are positively bedeviled with commitments and need to prepare a quick dish meant for sharing. After all, if you're all booked up for the day, how can you be expected to spend it in the kitchen?

INGREDIENTS

6 eggs
½ tsp baking soda
3 Tbsp mayonnaise
1 tsp Dijon mustard
1 Tbsp sriracha
Dash of Worcestershire sauce
⅛ tsp sea salt
⅛ tsp freshly ground black pepper
Smoked paprika, for serving

DIRECTIONS

1. Place the eggs in a medium saucepan and fill the pan with enough water so it covers the eggs by about an inch. Sprinkle the baking soda into the saucepan.

2. Bring the eggs to a boil over high heat, then remove the pan from the heat, cover with a lid and let stand for 9 minutes.

3. Drain the hot water from the saucepan and refill it with cold water to cool the eggs. When cooled, peel them under running water to remove all of the shell pieces.

4. Slice the eggs in half lengthwise and remove the yolks. Place the yolks in a food processor or small blender. Arrange the whites on a large plate or platter.

5. Add the mayonnaise, mustard, sriracha, Worcestershire sauce, salt, and pepper to the yolks. Blend until smooth. Taste and add additional seasoning if necessary.

6. Fill a piping bag fitted with a star tip with the yolk mixture. (Alternatively, fill a quart size freezer bag with the mixture and cut the tip off of one corner.)

7. Pipe the yolk mixture evenly into the egg white halves. If you don't find yourself rushing off to one of your many engagements, you can always spoon the mixture into the eggs.

8. Sprinkle with the paprika and serve.

MAKES 12 BEDEVILED EGGS

FRIPPET FRITTERS

Call them frivolous or flamboyant if you must, dear,
but whatever you do, don't start eating these without me.

INGREDIENTS

3 cups frozen corn kernels, thawed and drained
1 cup all-purpose flour
1 Tbsp sugar
1 tsp baking powder
¼ tsp garlic powder
½ tsp salt
¼ tsp pepper
2 large eggs, lightly beaten
¾ cup heavy cream
Vegetable oil, for frying
Flaky sea salt, for serving
Fresh chives, for serving
Sour cream or garlic aioli, for serving

DIRECTIONS

1. In a large bowl, combine the corn, flour, sugar, baking powder, garlic powder, salt, and pepper.

2. Stir in the eggs and heavy cream until the batter is well-combined.

3. Line a baking sheet with paper towels.

4. Coat the bottom of a large saute pan with ¼ inch vegetable oil and place it over medium-high heat.

5. Once the oil is hot, scoop 2- to 3-Tbsp mounds of the batter into the pan, spreading the batter lightly into a disc shape with the back of a metal spoon. Do not cook more than two to three fritters at a time.

6. Cook the fritters for 2 to 3 minutes or until golden brown, then flip and cook an additional 1 to 2 minutes until golden brown on both sides and cooked through.

7. Transfer fritters to the paper towel-lined baking sheet, season immediately with salt and repeat the cooking process with the remaining batter.

8. Sprinkle the fritters with chives and serve hot with sour cream or garlic aioli for dipping.

MAKES 12 FRITTERS

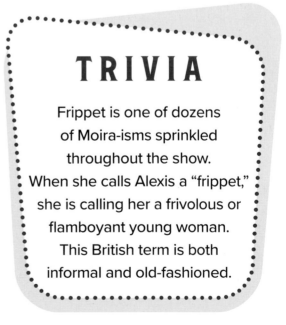

TRIVIA

Frippet is one of dozens of Moira-isms sprinkled throughout the show.
When she calls Alexis a "frippet," she is calling her a frivolous or flamboyant young woman.
This British term is both informal and old-fashioned.

GOAT CHEESE NOM NOMS

Nom nom for whomever gets to indulge in these perfectly sweet and savory bites. If you're not a fan of basil, rosemary makes an excellent substitute.

INGREDIENTS

- 2 oz soft goat cheese
- 12 buttery crackers, like Ritz
- 2 Tbsp blackberry jam
- 3 leaves fresh basil, thinly sliced into ribbons

DIRECTIONS

1. Let the goat cheese warm up on your kitchen counter until soft and spreadable.
2. Divide the goat cheese evenly and spread a bit of the cheese on each cracker using a butter knife.
3. Top each cracker with a small spoonful of the blackberry jam.
4. Garnish with the basil.

MAKES 12 NOM NOMS

TIPS AND TRICKS

The French word "chèvre," which means both "goat" and "goat cheese," is often used when referring to fresh goat cheeses.

MAYORAL FONDUE

Eschew the fondue forks and just use your fingers to dip your favorite morsels into this molten cheesy goodness. Be careful with the hunks of baguette though; they are slippery little bastards.

INGREDIENTS

- 1 lb shredded sharp cheddar cheese
- 1 Tbsp all-purpose flour
- ¾ cup lager beer
- 1 Tbsp minced garlic
- 1 Tbsp Worcestershire sauce
- 1½ tsp mustard powder

DIRECTIONS

1. In a large mixing bowl, combine the cheese and flour, mixing well.

2. In a medium saucepan over medium heat, bring the beer to a light boil and stir in remaining ingredients.

3. Gently fold the cheese mixture into the beer mixture.

4. Reduce the heat to low and stir the mixture until the cheese is melted, about 5 minutes. If the mixture is too thick, add more beer.

5. Serve with vegetables, Mall Pretzels (see pg. 102), apple slices, brats, or just lick it off of your hand.

MAKES 4 SERVINGS, OR ENOUGH FOR 1 HUNGRY MAYOR

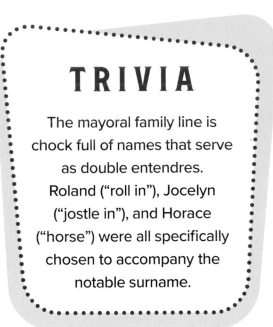

TRIVIA

The mayoral family line is chock full of names that serve as double entendres. Roland ("roll in"), Jocelyn ("jostle in"), and Horace ("horse") were all specifically chosen to accompany the notable surname.

LOVEBIRD WINGS

It's almost an impossible choice between the Lovers' Curry (pg. 56)
and Lovebird Wings, but the maple-sriracha glaze
makes these wings the clear winner.

INGREDIENTS

- 2 Tbsp baking powder
- 2 tsp kosher salt
- 1 tsp freshly ground black pepper
- 1 tsp smoked paprika
- 2½ lb whole chicken wing sections

MAPLE-SRIRACHA GLAZE

- ⅓ cup maple syrup
- ⅓ cup sriracha
- 1 Tbsp seasoned rice vinegar
- ¼ tsp sesame oil

DIRECTIONS

1. Preheat the oven to 425 degrees F.

2. Line a baking sheet with aluminum foil and place a wire rack over the foil. This will allow excess fat to run off during cooking.

3. In a small bowl, whisk together baking powder, salt, black pepper, and paprika. Place the whole chicken wings in a large bowl.

4. Sprinkle half of the spice mixture over the wings and toss to evenly coat. Sprinkle the remaining spice mixture over the wings and toss to coat again. Place the wings onto the rack of the prepared baking sheet.

5. Bake for 20 minutes. Use tongs to turn the wings and continue baking for 20 minutes.

Turn the wings again and bake until the wings are browned and crispy, about 5 minutes more. Transfer wings to a large bowl.

6. In a medium bowl, whisk together the glaze ingredients until smooth.

7. Drizzle the glaze over the wings and toss to coat. Serve immediately.

MAKES 4 SERVINGS

TIPS AND TRICKS

If you'd rather skip the sriracha but still love heat, swap it out for sambal oelek, a Southeast Asian sauce sure to fire up your taste buds.

SCHITT FAMILY CHEESE BALL

An easy cheese ball appetizer to serve to guests. Serve with your favorite crackers and crudites and enjoy! Keeps the love life percolating. For an extra flavorsome version, use bacon bits instead of chopped almonds (pictured).

INGREDIENTS

- 1 (1-oz) package ranch dressing mix
- 2½ cups shredded cheese of choice (cheddar, mozzarella, or pepper jack would be fine)
- 3 (8-oz) packages cream cheese, softened
- 1½ cups chopped almonds

DIRECTIONS

1. Either by hand or in a stand mixer, mix the ranch powder and shredded cheese into the cream cheese.

2. Scrape the mixture out of the bowl and onto a piece of plastic wrap. Use the plastic wrap to shape the mixture into a ball. Place the plastic-wrapped ball in the freezer for 15 minutes.

3. Unwrap the ball and roll it in the chopped almonds to coat.

4. Cover and refrigerate until ready to serve with a variety of crackers.

MAKES 6 SERVINGS

TRIVIA

Actress Jennifer Robertson wasn't really pregnant when her character Jocelyn was pregnant, so she wore a fake maternity belly in season 4. Actor Chris Elliott wore a prosthetic belly for his portrayal of Roland Schitt, an upgrade from the pillow he stuffed into his shirt for season 1.

LOVE THAT JOURNEY FOR YOU GUACAMOLE

Excellent choice to take to a small-town party, especially when Stavros is being a little B and posting pictures with other girls.

INGREDIENTS

3 avocados

Juice of 1 lime

1 tsp kosher salt

½ cup diced onion

¼ cup chopped fresh cilantro

1 medium tomato, diced

1 tsp minced garlic

DIRECTIONS

1. Halve the avocados. Remove the pits and scoop the flesh into a medium bowl.

2. Add the lime juice and salt and mash together well.

3. Mix in the onion, cilantro, tomatoes, and garlic.

4. Serve immediately or refrigerate in an airtight container for up to three days.

MAKES 4 SERVINGS

TIPS AND TRICKS

As a world traveler, Alexis would likely recommend preparing and serving guacamole in a traditional Mexican molcajete.

MURDER MYSTERY BAKED BRIE

This sweet and savory appetizer is guaranteed to keep your guests (and potential murderers) from going hungry, no matter how long the party goes.

INGREDIENTS

- 1 sheet puff pastry (thawed according to package directions if frozen)
- 1 (8-oz) round or wedge brie cheese (do not remove rind)
- 2 Tbsp raspberry jam
- 1 tsp brown sugar
- 2 Tbsp slivered or chopped almonds
- 1 egg, beaten

DIRECTIONS

1. Preheat the oven to 375 degrees F.

2. On a lined baking sheet, lay out the puff pastry.

3. Place the brie round or wedge on top of the dough.

4. Spread the jam on the brie, then top with the brown sugar and almonds.

5. Fold the dough over the top of the cheese, making sure to pinch the dough well when folding so the brie stays in the pastry while it bakes. Trim off the excess dough.

6. Using a pastry brush, brush the top and sides of the pastry with the beaten egg.

7. Bake for 30 minutes until golden brown. Cool for 10 minutes. Serve with crackers or apple slices.

MAKES 6 SERVINGS

TIPS AND TRICKS

This baked brie can be enjoyed on its own, or paired with a charcuterie board and your favorite white wine for a truly decadent spread.

BLOUSE BARN BRUSCHETTA

A little flirty, a little sassy, these appetizers are an excellent choice to serve while wearing your most stylish blouse. Some call these bruschetta toasts "upscale" and "high end," but David thinks they're a bit skanky.

INGREDIENTS

- ¼ cup fresh basil, stems removed, cut into ribbons
- ½ cup sun-dried tomatoes packed in oil, chopped
- 6 Roma (plum) tomatoes, chopped
- 3 cloves minced garlic
- ¼ cup olive oil
- 2 Tbsp balsamic vinegar
- ¼ tsp salt
- ¼ tsp ground black pepper
- 1 baguette, cut into ¾-inch slices
- 2 cups shredded mozzarella or jack cheese

DIRECTIONS

1. Preheat the oven on the broiler setting.

2. Add the basil, sun-dried tomatoes, Roma tomatoes, garlic, olive oil, vinegar, salt, and pepper to a large mixing bowl. Allow to sit for 15 minutes.

3. On a baking sheet, arrange the baguette slices in a single layer. Broil for 1 to 2 minutes until lightly browned.

4. Remove from the oven. Divide the tomato mixture evenly over the baguette slices. Top with shredded cheese.

5. Broil for 3 to 5 minutes, watching the toasts. The cheese should be melted but not burnt.

MAKES 6 SERVINGS

TRIVIA

Catherine O'Hara and Robin Duke (Blouse Barn Wendy) went to high school together at Burnhamthorpe Collegiate Institute in Etobicoke, Ontario.

Half Combo,
pg. 70

MAINS

WHEN HUNGER'S GOT YOU "ACTING LIKE A DISGRUNTLED PELICAN," THESE MEALS WILL SATE EVEN THE MOST RAVENOUS APPETITE.

BETTER THAN YOUR EX ANNIVERSARY SLIDERS

One needn't be a grillmaster to be successful with these sliders. Add macaroni salad, potato salad, and beers for a celebratory cookout. Makes enough food for the whole family, plus a rogue ex-fiancée.

INGREDIENTS

- 2 lb ground beef (80/20)
- 1 envelope dry onion soup mix
- 2 Tbsp Worcestershire sauce
- 2 Tbsp ketchup
- 2 (12-packs) Original Hawaiian Sweet Rolls, halved

DIRECTIONS

1. Preheat the grill. In a large bowl, combine the ground beef, soup mix, Worcestershire, and ketchup.

2. Form the slider patties by grabbing a small chunk of the ground beef and shaping into a disc using your hands. Let rest at least 10 minutes before grilling.

3. Throw the patties on the grill and cook for about 2 to 3 minutes per side. If adding cheese, do so during the last minute of grilling and keep the grill closed.

4. Serve sliders with your choice of toppings. Best eaten with lots of sides while crying in your motel room.

MAKES 16 SLIDERS

TRIVIA

Stacey Farber, the actress who plays Patrick's ex-fiancée Rachel, is a real-life friend of Dan Levy.

FOLD IN THE CHEESE AAAHNCHILADAS

Just like your mother's recipe. What does "fold in the cheese" mean?
You fold it in. I cannot show you everything.

INGREDIENTS

2   Tbsp butter
⅔   cup yellow onion, chopped
2   Tbsp all-purpose flour
1½ cups chicken broth
1   cup chopped green chiles (canned are fine)
2   cloves minced garlic
¾   tsp salt
2   dashes ground cumin
1   cup shredded Monterey Jack cheese
1   cup shredded mild cheddar cheese
12 (8-inch) corn tortillas
    Canola oil for frying
2   cups cooked and shredded chicken
1   cup heavy cream
¼   cup chopped green onion
½   cup sliced olives, optional
1   pint cherry tomatoes
    Salsa, for serving

DIRECTIONS

1. In a saucepan over medium heat, melt the butter.
2. Add the onion and saute until soft, about 5 minutes, then stir in the flour.
3. Add the broth, chiles, garlic, salt, and cumin. Reduce heat and simmer for about 15 minutes. Remove from heat.

4. Take ¼ cup of each of the cheeses, setting the rest aside for filling and topping. Fold in the cheese. *Just fold it in.*
5. Preheat the oven to 350 degrees F.
6. In a cast iron skillet or Dutch oven with about half an inch of canola oil, lightly fry the tortillas. Don't fry them too crispy because they will need to be rolled.
7. Dunk each tortilla in the sauce, thinly coating both sides. Combine the cheeses in a bowl, reserving a half cup for the top.
8. Place 2 heaping Tbsp of chicken and about 2 Tbsp of cheese in the center of each tortilla. Roll and place seam-side down in a shallow ovenproof dish.
9. Pour the remaining sauce over the tortillas, then cover evenly with heavy cream. Sprinkle the remaining ½ cup cheese mixture and green onions over the top.
10. Bake uncovered for 20 minutes.
11. Serve immediately, garnished with the olives, cherry tomatoes, and salsa on the side.

MAKES 8 SERVINGS

TRIVIA

Moira's accent— a bit British, a bit Mid-Atlantic, and a bit Canadian—was a creative choice from Catherine O'Hara, who endeavored to sound a bit unhuman. Two books that informed her unique vocabulary are *Foyle's Philavery: A Treasury of Unusual Words* and *Mrs. Byrne's Dictionary*.

ROLAND'S WAFFLES AND
FRIED CHICKEN WITH EXTRA SKINS

This is so good, it's no wonder it's "the usual."
Add hot sauce and butter to serve this meal the Rollie way.

INGREDIENTS

 3 eggs
¼ cup heavy cream
 2 tsp cayenne pepper
 2 Tbsp salt, divided
 1 Tbsp ground black pepper
1⅓ cups all-purpose flour
⅔ cup cornstarch
 1 quart neutral oil for frying
 8 chicken tenderloins
½ cup mayonnaise
 2 Tbsp real maple syrup
 1 Tbsp yellow mustard
12 slices bacon
 8 plain frozen waffles
 8 thin slices cheddar
   Hot sauce, to taste
   Butter, for serving

DIRECTIONS

1. In a large bowl, whisk together eggs, cream, cayenne, 1 Tbsp salt, and black pepper.
2. In a paper bag, shake to combine the flour, cornstarch, and 1 Tbsp salt.
3. Dip the chicken into the egg mixture, then place the chicken into the flour mixture and shake the bag to coat.
4. Arrange breaded chicken on a wire rack in one layer. Let the chicken rest for 20 minutes to allow the coating to set.
5. Heat a couple inches of oil in a deep-fryer or large saucepan to 375 degrees F. In small batches, fry the chicken 5 to 7 minutes until golden brown. Remove the chicken, then drain on a plate lined with paper towels. Keep warm in the oven at 275 degrees F.
NOTE: If you happen to have extra chicken skins handy, fry in the same manner. Cook until golden brown. They will not take as long to fry up as the full pieces of chicken, so take care that they don't burn. Not that Rollie wouldn't eat them anyway, but still.
6. Mix mayonnaise, maple syrup, and mustard in a medium bowl. Set aside.
7. In a large dry skillet over medium-high heat, fry bacon until lightly browned, turning frequently, about 8 to 10 minutes. Do not overcook, as the bacon will cook more in the oven. Drain on a paper towel-lined plate.
8. Preheat oven to 375 degrees F.
9. To assemble the chicken sandwiches, place eight frozen waffles on a baking sheet. Parbake the waffles for 2 minutes, then remove from the oven.
10. Top four of the waffles with two chicken tenders. On the remaining four waffles, add three slices of bacon. Top all eight waffles with a slice of cheese.

TRIVIA

Chris Elliott, the actor who portrays Roland Schitt, is one of the very few Americans in the cast. Almost everyone is Canadian!

11. Broil the waffles for 2 to 3 minutes so the cheese is melted and bubbly.

12. Spoon 2 Tbsp of the sauce on the waffles with chicken, followed by hot sauce to taste.

13. Top each chicken side with a bacon side. Serve immediately.

MAKES 4 SANDWICHES

LOVERS' CURRY

If you can survive the awkward honeymoon attention,
fake marriage will be a piece of cake.
It doesn't have actual lovebirds in it, just chicken.

INGREDIENTS

- 2 lb boneless, skinless chicken breasts
- 3 tsp salt, divided
- ½ cup cooking oil
- 1½ cups onion, chopped
- 1 Tbsp minced garlic
- 1½ tsp minced fresh ginger
- 1 Tbsp curry powder
- 1 tsp ground cumin
- 1 tsp ground turmeric
- 1 tsp ground coriander
- 1 tsp cayenne pepper
- 1 Tbsp water
- 1 (15-oz) can crushed tomatoes
- 1 cup plain yogurt
- 2 Tbsp chopped fresh cilantro, divided
- ½ cup chicken broth
- 1 tsp garam masala
- 1 lemon wedge

DIRECTIONS

1. Sprinkle the chicken breasts with 2 tsp of salt.

2. In a large skillet over high heat, warm the oil. Cook the chicken in batches until completely browned, about 4 to 6 minutes. Remove the chicken to drain on a plate lined with paper towels.

3. Using the same skillet, reduce the heat to medium-high. Cook the onion, garlic, and ginger until the onion turns translucent, stirring constantly, about 8 minutes.

4. Add the curry powder, cumin, turmeric, coriander, cayenne, and 1 Tbsp of water to the skillet. Cook for 1 minute, stirring constantly.

5. Mix in the tomatoes, yogurt, 1 Tbsp cilantro, and remaining tsp of salt.

6. Return the chicken to the skillet along with any juices on the plate.

7. Pour broth into the mixture and bring to a boil. Stir well, thoroughly coating the chicken with sauce.

8. Sprinkle the garam masala and 1 Tbsp cilantro over the chicken. Cover with lid and let simmer until the chicken breasts are no longer pink in the center and the juices run clear, about 20 minutes, or until its internal temperature reaches 165 degrees F on an instant-read thermometer.

9. Squeeze a lemon wedge over the curry. Enjoy over rice with your new fake spouse.

MAKES 6 SERVINGS

TRIVIA

Schitt's Creek has attracted attention from quite a few celebrity fans. Dan Levy said he cried and had a panic attack when Mariah Carey tweeted about the show.

JOHNNY'S CHRISTMAS MEATLOAF

I didn't want to say anything, but Meatloaf Night was yesterday.

INGREDIENTS

- 2 eggs
- ⅔ cup milk
- 2 tsp salt
- ½ tsp ground black pepper
- 3 slices bread, crumbled
- 1½ lb ground beef
- 1 yellow onion, minced
- 1 cup shredded cheddar cheese
- ½ cup shredded carrot
- ¼ cup brown sugar
- ¼ cup ketchup
- 1 Tbsp yellow mustard

DIRECTIONS

1. Preheat the oven to 350 degrees F.

2. In a large bowl, whisk the eggs, milk, salt, and black pepper.

3. Add breadcrumbs and stir until the liquid has been absorbed.

4. Mix the ground beef, onion, cheese, and carrots into the bread mixture, ensuring the meat is completely broken up. Scoop the mixture into a 9-by-5-inch loaf pan and press the mixture into the pan.

5. In a small bowl, combine the brown sugar, ketchup, and mustard, then stir until the sugar has dissolved. Spread evenly over the meatloaf.

6. Bake uncovered for 60 minutes, then check the temperature. Bake until the middle of the meatloaf is at least 160 degrees F. Serve with eggnog.

MAKES 6 SERVINGS

TIPS AND TRICKS

Meatloaf can also be made with lamb, pork, veal, venison, poultry, and even seafood, often in combination, so find what suits your palate.

JOCELYN'S DORITO CASSEROLE

The two words in the English language that bring people the most joy: Dorito Casserole. You don't need to be pregnant to crave this terrific dish, but it certainly helps.

INGREDIENTS

- 1 (14.5-oz) bag Nacho Cheese Doritos, crushed
- 3 cups chopped cooked chicken
- 1 (15.25-oz) can corn, drained
- 2 cups shredded Mexican cheese blend, divided
- 1½ cups salsa
- 1 (10.75-oz) can condensed cream of mushroom soup
- 1 (10.75-oz) can condensed cream of chicken soup
- 8 oz sour cream

DIRECTIONS

1. Preheat the oven to 350 degrees F. Lightly grease a 9-by-13-inch baking dish.

2. Cover the bottom of the prepared baking dish with half of the crushed Doritos.

3. In a large bowl, mix together the chicken, corn, 1 cup cheese, salsa, soups, and sour cream. Fold in the remaining crushed chips.

4. Pour the chicken mixture over crushed chips into the baking dish.

5. Bake for 20 minutes, then remove.

6. Spread the remaining 1 cup of cheese over the casserole and increase the oven temperature to 375 degrees F.

7. Bake until the cheese is melted and bubbling, about 10 additional minutes.

8. Let cool for 5 minutes. Serve alongside a green salad or something light to balance out this dish, I beg of you.

MAKES 12 SERVINGS

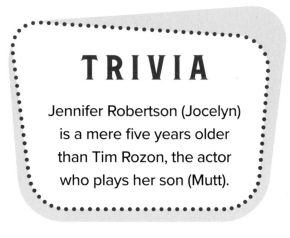

TRIVIA

Jennifer Robertson (Jocelyn) is a mere five years older than Tim Rozon, the actor who plays her son (Mutt).

ONE SINGULAR PIZZA

What is this, *Les Miz*? This meal should be shared, because this certainly isn't some all-one-can-consume smörgåsbord.

INGREDIENTS

- 6 oz thick-cut bacon, chopped
- 1 lb pizza dough
- ½ medium red apple (such as Pink Lady), cored and thinly sliced
- ½ medium tart apple (such as Granny Smith), cored and thinly sliced
- 1½ cups shredded sharp cheddar
- 2 tsp fresh thyme leaves
  Pure maple syrup, for drizzling

DIRECTIONS

1. Place a pizza stone in the oven and preheat oven to 500 degrees F.

2. In a skillet over medium heat, cook the bacon until it browns at the edges, about 4 to 6 minutes. Be careful not to let it get too crispy, as it will continue cooking in the oven.

3. Remove the skillet from the heat and transfer the bacon to a paper towel-lined plate to drain. Reserve the bacon grease in the pan.

4. Stretch the dough out into a 12-inch circle. Remove the hot stone from the oven and place the dough on top. Brush the dough lightly with some of the reserved bacon grease.

5. Arrange the apple slices on top of the dough in a single layer. Scatter the bacon over the apples and top with the cheese.

6. Bake until the crust is golden and the cheese has melted, approximately 6 to 8 minutes.

7. Remove pizza from the oven. While the pizza is still hot, sprinkle with the thyme and drizzle the maple syrup. Slice and serve immediately.

MAKES 4 SERVINGS

TRIVIA

Dan Levy's favorite pizza is pepperoni with double cheese.

SLOPPY JOCELYNS

These are hands-down the best thing to serve if you're trying to woo an investor. Bill and Melinda Gates would love them. Serve these on store-bought hamburger buns with sesame seeds to go all out.

INGREDIENTS

- 1 Tbsp olive oil
- ½ cup white onion, minced
- 1 lb lean ground beef
- ½ tsp garlic powder
- 1 tsp prepared yellow mustard
- ¾ cup ketchup
- Salt and pepper to taste
- Hamburger buns

DIRECTIONS

1. In a skillet with oil over medium heat, cook the onion until it becomes translucent and starts to brown, about 5 to 6 minutes.
2. Add the ground beef to the onions and cook until the beef has browned evenly, about 5 minutes. Drain any excess fat.
3. Stir in the garlic powder, mustard, and ketchup and mix. Reduce heat to low and simmer for 5 minutes.
4. Season with salt and pepper and serve on hamburger buns.

MAKES 6 SERVINGS

TRIVIA

Jocelyn's tongue-in-cheek renaming of the classic cafeteria staple isn't the only alternate title for Sloppy Joes. Depending on the decade and region, they have also been called Spanish Hamburgers, Toasted Devil Hamburgers, or Beef Mironton.

THERE'S A DEAD GUY IN
ROOM FOUR-CHEESE MACARONI

The perfect comfort dish after you have endured a cornucopia of trauma, this cheesy pasta will have you going back for seconds while trying to hide it from the guests.

INGREDIENTS

- 2 cups elbow macaroni
- 4 Tbsp unsalted butter
- ⅓ cup all-purpose flour
- 2 cups milk
- 4 oz processed cheese product
- ½ tsp onion powder
- 1 tsp garlic powder
- ⅛ tsp cayenne pepper
- ½ tsp paprika
- 1 tsp salt
- ½ tsp pepper
- ¼ cup white onion, minced
- 3 oz shredded cheddar cheese
- 3 oz shredded Swiss cheese
- 3 oz shredded Gruyere cheese

DIRECTIONS

1. Preheat the oven to 350 degrees F.
2. Lightly grease a 9-by-13-inch baking dish and set aside. Prepare the elbow macaroni to al dente according to the package directions.
3. In a medium saucepan, melt the butter over medium heat, about 2 minutes. Stir in the flour to make a roux.
4. When the mixture is cream-colored and thick, pour in the milk and stir constantly until the mixture comes to a rolling boil, about 1

minute. Remove from heat.
5. Add the processed cheese, seasonings, salt, and pepper. Stir until the cheese is fully melted and set aside. This sauce will be poured over the dish.
6. Add macaroni, onion, and shredded cheeses to the baking dish and gently stir together. Pour the reserved cheese sauce on top, making sure to reach every corner of the dish.
7. Cover and bake at 350 degrees F for 45 minutes. Let cool slightly before serving.

MAKES 8 SERVINGS

TRIVIA

Catherine O'Hara and Eugene Levy have been co-stars across five decades. They began working together on *SCTV*, a Canadian sketch comedy show, in the 1970s.

TURKEY SHOOT SANDWICH

Elton John used to host an annual hunt at his place, but it was more about the lunch. Although this sandwich would have been a little lowbrow for Elton, it's a great way to use up Thanksgiving leftovers.

INGREDIENTS

Butter, for spreading

Two slices white bread

3 Tbsp whipped cream cheese

2 Tbsp cranberry sauce

3 oz turkey, sliced or shredded

DIRECTIONS

1. Butter the outside of each slice of bread. Heat a frying pan over medium heat.

2. Place the bread slices butter-side down into the hot skillet.

3. On each slice of bread, spread half of the cream cheese and half of the cranberry sauce.

4. Top one slice with the turkey.

5. Flip the slice of bread without the turkey on top of the other slice. Grill the sandwich on each side until the bread has turned a deep golden brown and the center is warm throughout. Serve.

MAKES 1 SANDWICH

TRIVIA

Despite what we see in season 1, episode 7 if you are hunting turkey with a shotgun, it technically is good placement to aim for the bird's head and neck. However, if you are using a bow to hunt, it is best to aim for the heart/lungs to kill the animal quickly.

HALF COMBO

The combo of the day is butternut squash soup paired with an apple and brie sandwich. Listen, don't make this too complicated. It's just a cup of soup and half a sandwich. There is no full combo, no evolution of the combo, and don't you dare bring up the brisket.

INGREDIENTS

SOUP

- 1 (2-lb) butternut squash, halved and deseeded
- 1 Tbsp olive oil
- 4 cups chicken broth
- 2 Tbsp butter
- 1 cup diced onion
- 4 cloves garlic, minced
- 2 tsp curry powder
- 1 tsp salt
- ½ tsp ground cumin
- ¼ tsp cayenne pepper
- ½ cup half-and-half
- 2 Tbsp maple syrup or honey
- ¼ cup sour cream, optional

SANDWICH

- 1–2 Tbsp butter, softened
- 2 slices sourdough bread
- 2 oz brie, sliced
- ¼ tsp fresh thyme leaves
  Pinch cracked black pepper
- 6 thin slices apple (Honeycrisp or similar)
  Pinch sea salt
  Honey, for drizzling

DIRECTIONS

SOUP

1. Preheat the oven to 400 degrees F.

2. Coat the squash in olive oil. Roast cut side down on a foil-lined baking sheet for 50 minutes or until soft.

3. Once the squash has cooled, scoop out the flesh into a medium saucepan. Add the broth and simmer on medium-low heat for 10 minutes, stirring occasionally.

4. In a separate large pot over medium heat, melt the butter, about 1 to 2 minutes. Add the onion and garlic and cook until softened and browned, stirring often, about 10 to 15

TRIVIA

Sarah Levy (Twyla Sands) is the real-life younger sister of Dan Levy (David). Dan is three years older.

minutes. Add the curry powder, salt, cumin, cayenne and the squash mixture and bring to a boil, then reduce heat to low. Simmer for 10 minutes and remove from heat.

5. Using an immersion blender, blend soup to desired consistency. Alternatively, wait for the soup to cool before pulsing in a blender.

6. Stir in the half-and-half and maple syrup. Add sour cream to taste just before serving.

SANDWICH

1. Butter the outside of each slice of bread. Heat a frying pan over medium heat.

2. Place the bread butter-side down in the hot skillet. Arrange the cheese slices on top of each piece. Sprinkle with thyme and cracked black pepper.

3. On one slice of bread, arrange the apple slices in a single layer. Top with a pinch of salt and a drizzle of honey.

4. Flip the slice of bread without apples on top of the other slice and continue grilling the sandwich on each side until the bread has turned a deep golden brown and the cheese has melted through.

MAKES 6–8 SERVINGS OF SOUP AND 1 SANDWICH

WRITE-OFF RISOTTO

Yes, high quality Parmesan can be expensive, but don't worry, it's a write-off. You simply visit your local cheesemonger or neighborhood apothecary, find a cheese you fancy, and the government will write it off!

INGREDIENTS

- 6 cups low-sodium chicken broth
- 1 Tbsp olive oil
- 1 medium onion, chopped
- 1½ cups Arborio rice
- ½ cup dry white wine
- ¾ tsp salt
  Freshly ground black pepper
- 3 lightly packed cups baby spinach
- 1 cup frozen peas
- ½ lb asparagus, steamed and chopped into bite-sized pieces
- ¼ cup freshly grated Parmesan

DIRECTIONS

1. In a medium saucepan over medium heat, bring the broth to a simmer, about 3 to 4 minutes or until you see small bubbles forming.

2. In a heavy saucepan over moderately low heat, heat the oil and cook the onion, stirring occasionally, until soft, for 3 to 5 minutes.

3. Add the rice and cook, stirring constantly, for 1 minute.

4. Add wine and simmer, stirring constantly, until absorbed, about 1 minute.

5. Add ¾ cup of the hot broth, the salt and a few grinds of fresh pepper. Simmer, stirring constantly, until broth is absorbed, about 2 to 3 minutes. Continue simmering and adding hot broth, about ¾ cup at a time, stirring constantly and allowing the broth to be absorbed before adding more, until rice is almost tender and creamy-looking, about 18 minutes.

TRIVIA

While it was clear David didn't have much of a grasp on tax write-offs, his success with Rose Apothecary did inspire an off-screen version of Monopoly. Fans can play a *Schitt's Creek* version of the classic game. While there are no top hats or Scottie dogs, you can play as a Bébé Crow, Rosebud Motel Key, David's Sunglasses, or Moira's Wig.

6. Add the spinach and peas and cook until the spinach is wilted, about 1 to 2 minutes.

7. Add the asparagus and cook just until the vegetables are hot, about 2 to 3 minutes.

8. Stir in the Parmesan and add more broth if the risotto seems too thick.

MAKES 4 SERVINGS

PREORDERED TUNA MELT

Eat this classic diner-style tuna melt hot,
you know these things turn on a dime.

INGREDIENTS

  1 (5-oz) can tuna, drained
1½ Tbsp mayonnaise
  1 Tbsp butter
  2 slices sourdough bread
  2 slices Swiss cheese

DIRECTIONS

1. In a small mixing bowl, combine the tuna and the mayonnaise.

2. Butter the outside of each slice of bread.

3. On the first slice of bread, layer one piece of Swiss cheese, then the tuna mixture. Top with the remaining slice of cheese and bread.

4. Heat a frying pan over medium heat and add the sandwich when the pan is hot.

5. Grill the sandwich on each side until the bread has turned a deep golden brown and the cheese has melted.

6. Cut the sandwich on a diagonal and plate up. Best enjoyed immediately.

MAKES 1 SANDWICH

TRIVIA

Another father-daughter team almost made it into the *Schitt's Creek* cast: Chris Elliott's daughter, Abby, portrayed Alexis in one version of the pilot episode.

ANNUAL BEEFCAKE

This hearty cottage pie is sure to please animals, lovers,
your cousin Dwayne, people who hate their jobs,
and anyone in a loveless marriage.

INGREDIENTS

TOPPING

1½ lb potatoes, peeled and cubed
 2 tsp salt
 2 Tbsp salted butter
 ¼ cup milk
 ½ cup sour cream
 2 cups shredded cheddar cheese

FILLING

 1 Tbsp olive oil, divided
 2 lb lean ground beef, divided
 1 tsp salt, divided
 ¼ tsp pepper, divided
 1 medium onion, diced
 3 cloves garlic, minced
 2 tsp fresh thyme
 1 (16-oz) bag frozen mixed vegetables
 ¼ cup tomato paste
 ¾ cup stout
 1 Tbsp Worcestershire sauce
 ½ cup beef broth

DIRECTIONS

1. In a large pot, add the potatoes and cover
with water.

2. Add 2 tsp of salt and boil over medium-high
heat until the potatoes are soft, about 10 to 12
minutes. Drain the water from the pot.

3. Add butter, milk, and sour cream. Mash
until smooth. Cover and set aside.

4. Preheat the oven to 350 degrees F.

5. In a large pan over medium-high heat, add
½ Tbsp of olive oil to half of the beef. Sprinkle
with half of the salt and pepper. Brown the

TRIVIA

In season 2, episode 8 when
Ted rolls back into town on a
motorcycle and encounters
Alexis while she's walking
outside, the actor on the bike
isn't really Dustin Milligan!
Turns out they're a stunt
double, but a quick cut
reveals Ted after his
helmet is taken off.

meat, breaking it up with a wooden spoon so that it cooks evenly.

6. Transfer to a dish while you cook the rest of the meat in the same way.

7. In the same pan, heat the remaining ½ Tbsp oil over medium and add the onion, garlic, and thyme. Cook until the onions become translucent and soft, about 5 minutes.

8. Add the beef, frozen vegetables, tomato paste, stout, Worcestershire sauce, and broth. Mix to combine. Let the mixture simmer for 5 to 7 minutes or until half of the liquid has been absorbed or boiled down. The alcohol will boil off during this step.

9. Pour the beef mixture into a 9-by-11-inch casserole dish or 11-inch round casserole dish. Spread evenly over the bottom.

10. Top the beef mixture with the mashed potatoes, using a spoon to create small peaks in the mashed potatoes.

11. Bake for 20 minutes. Top the beefcake with the shredded cheddar and broil for several minutes until the top is golden brown. Remove from the oven and let rest 10 minutes.

MAKES 8 SERVINGS

HUNGRY HUNGRY HIPPO LASAGNA

This delicious autumnal lasagna may not be the best
post-tooth extraction meal, but it makes for a satisfying dinner
served alongside crusty bread and a green salad.

INGREDIENTS

- 2 sweet potatoes, peeled and diced
- 1 Tbsp olive oil
- ½ tsp garlic powder
- ½ tsp dried thyme
- 1½ cups shredded mozzarella cheese or more
- 10 oz lasagna noodles
- ½ cup Parmesan cheese
- ½ tsp Italian seasoning
- ¼ tsp basil

BUTTERNUT SAUCE

- 2 cups butternut squash puree
- 1 cup ricotta cheese
- ½ cup milk or more, if needed
- ½ tsp salt
- ¼ tsp nutmeg
- ½ tsp cayenne

SPINACH FILLING

- 10 oz frozen spinach, thawed
- 1 cup ricotta cheese
- 1 cup shredded mozzarella cheese
- 3 garlic cloves, minced
- ½ tsp salt
- ¼ tsp freshly ground black pepper
- ½ tsp dried basil

DIRECTIONS

1. Preheat the oven to 450 degrees F.
2. Toss the sweet potatoes with olive oil, garlic powder, and thyme. Roast for 20 minutes or until just soft.
3. While the sweet potatoes are cooking, prepare the sauce. In a large bowl or food processor, combine all sauce ingredients. Taste and adjust seasonings as necessary.
4. Now, prepare the filling. In a medium bowl, combine the spinach, ricotta cheese, mozzarella, garlic, salt, pepper, and dried basil. Taste and adjust seasonings as necessary.

TRIVIA

Blue shirts are a wardrobe staple for Patrick (Noah Reid), but post-tooth extraction in season 6 episode 5, he is notably wearing a dark gray hooded sweatshirt.

5. Remove the sweet potatoes from the oven and set aside. Reduce the oven temperature to 350 degrees F.

6. In a 9-by-11-inch pan, layer the lasagna as follows:

- ⅓ of the butternut sauce
- Sprinkle of mozzarella
- Layer of noodles
- ½ of the spinach filling
- ½ of the sweet potatoes
- Sprinkle of mozzarella
- Layer of noodles

7. Repeat this pattern again and cover the final layer of noodles with the remaining sauce. Top with the remaining mozzarella, Parmesan, Italian seasoning, and basil.

8. Cover with foil and bake for 30 minutes.

9. Remove the foil and bake for an additional 10 minutes to brown the cheese. Let cool slightly before serving.

MAKES 8 SERVINGS

A BIG PIECE OF FISH

This is best served with a bowl of room-temperature hollandaise.
If you aren't battling a vicious hangover, however, it pairs well with the
Happy Ending Massaged Kale Salad on pg. 100.

INGREDIENTS

¾ tsp sea salt
1 tsp brown sugar
½ tsp freshly ground black pepper
½ tsp garlic powder
½ tsp dried basil
½ tsp paprika
1 lb salmon filet
1 Tbsp butter
Squeeze of lemon

DIRECTIONS

1. Preheat the oven to 400 degrees F. Line a baking sheet with aluminum foil.
2. In a small bowl, combine the dry ingredients.
3. Place the filet on the baking sheet. Cover the top of the filet with the spice mixture and gently press it down onto the filet.
4. In a microwave-safe mug, heat the butter in 10-second intervals until melted. Drizzle the melted butter over the salmon.
5. Bake for 11 to 13 minutes.
6. Use a knife to check the salmon for doneness at the thickest part of the filet. It should look nearly opaque and the layers within the salmon should flake apart easily.
7. Top with a squeeze of fresh lemon.

MAKES 4 SERVINGS

TIPS AND TRICKS

The USDA recommends cooking fish to an internal temperature of 145 degrees F. When in doubt, use an instant-read thermometer.

SELFISH TACOS

These fish tacos will make you feel like you're on vacation, or at least somewhere better than a motel room that smells like a gym bag.

INGREDIENTS
CILANTRO-LIME CREMA
1 clove garlic
½ cup cilantro
2 Tbsp mayonnaise
¼ tsp chili powder
½ cup Greek yogurt or sour cream
  Zest and juice of 1 lime

TACOS
1 cup all-purpose flour, plus ½ cup for dredging
2 Tbsp cornstarch
1 tsp baking powder
½ tsp salt
1 egg
1 cup beer (lager, pale ale, etc.)
1 quart frying oil
1 lb cod fillets, cut into bite-sized pieces
1 package corn tortillas
½ medium head cabbage, finely shredded
1 avocado, sliced

DIRECTIONS
1. In a blender, combine all of the crema ingredients and pulse until smooth. Refrigerate until serving.
2. In a large bowl, add 1 cup flour, cornstarch, baking powder, and salt. In a separate medium bowl, whisk together the egg and beer.
3. Whisk the beer mixture into the flour mixture until smooth (a few small lumps are okay.)
4. Cover the bottom of a heavy saucepan with 1 to 2 inches of oil. Set the heat to medium-high. Using a thermometer, heat to 375 degrees F. Line a plate with paper towels and set aside.
5. Place the remaining ½ cup flour in a shallow bowl for dredging. Dip the fish pieces in flour and tap to remove excess. Coat each piece of fish in the batter and fry until golden brown, 3 to 5 minutes. Place the fish on the paper towel-lined plate to drain.
6. In another skillet, warm the tortillas.
7. To serve, place an equal amount of cabbage and fish into each tortilla, then a slice of avocado. Top with the crema.

MAKES 4 SERVINGS

TRIVIA

Schitt's Creek was the first time the father and son duo Eugene and Dan Levy worked together professionally (as Johnny and David, respectively).

STAVROS' SOUVLAKI

Why gallivant around the world with your dumb, shipping heir, loser boyfriend when these classic kebabs can give you a taste of Greece at home?

INGREDIENTS

2   lb chicken thighs
3   Tbsp olive oil
2   lemons, juiced
2   Tbsp oregano
1   Tbsp thyme
1   clove garlic, grated
    Zest of 1 lemon
    Sea salt and pepper to taste
    Fresh tzatziki, to serve

DIRECTIONS

1. In a large gallon-sized freezer bag, combine all ingredients except chicken and mix well.
2. Add the chicken to the bag. Shake well and let marinate for 30 minutes in the refrigerator. Soak wooden skewers (if using) for 30 minutes.
3. Preheat the grill. Thread 5 to 6 cubes of chicken onto each skewer.
4. Place the skewers on the preheated grill and cook for about 5 to 6 minutes on each side until cooked through.
5. Remove the skewers from the grill and serve with fresh tzatziki.

MAKES 4 SERVINGS

TRIVIA

Over the course of the series, Alexis' romantic past is painted by a series of offhand remarks about rich and famous people she has dated. Some notable flames mentioned include Prince Harry, Leonardo DiCaprio, and all three Hanson brothers.

BABY SPRINKLE BRANZINO

If you can't find an old contact to express-ship you a branzino in time for the Sprinkle you're planning, you can whip up this herbaceous version in your own oven.

INGREDIENTS

- ½ tsp kosher salt
- ½ tsp pepper
- ¼ tsp red pepper flakes
- 1–1½ lb whole branzino, scaled and gutted
- Extra-virgin olive oil
- 2 lemons (1 sliced into thin rounds, 1 cut into 6 wedges)
- 1 small bunch thyme sprigs
- Sprig of rosemary

DIRECTIONS

1. Preheat the oven to 450 degrees F.

2. Add the salt, pepper, and red pepper flakes to a small bowl and mix.

3. Pat the fish dry with a paper towel. Drizzle the fish with olive oil, then rub to lightly coat the interior cavity and the skin. Season with the spice mixture.

4. Place the lemon slices, thyme, and rosemary in the cavity of the fish. Stand the fish upright on a lined baking sheet, using the lemon wedges as wedges between the pan and the fish.

5. Bake until the fish is just cooked and flaky, 17 to 22 minutes.

6. Filet the fish and serve with a squeeze of lemon juice from the roasted lemon wedges.

MAKES 2 SERVINGS

TRIVIA

The game "Sleepy Mommy" was played in the episode "Baby Sprinkle" (S4E10) where pretend pills are tossed into Jocelyn's mouth. It was Dan Levy's idea, inspired by what he thought the character Moira Rose would have been like as a new mother.

FOLDING IN THE CHEESE

PERHAPS THE MOST iconic food moment in all of *Schitt's Creek* transpires in "Family Dinner" (season 2, episode 2), as Moira and David attempt to make enchiladas together. Their lack of cooking skills is highlighted when they demonstrate their unfamiliarity with "folding in" an ingredient. While folding in ingredients is not complicated, a novice in the kitchen may not have encountered a recipe calling for this technique, and therefore might be as confused as the Roses. Fear not: You can do this.

WHY FOLD?

Folding in ingredients preserves lightness. The technique typically appears in baking recipes more than in cooking recipes and the most common ingredients to be folded in include whipped egg whites, whipped cream, or whipped evaporated milk. Folding as opposed to stirring optimizes the amount of air in a mixture during the incorporation of additional ingredients. It is usually done in two to three rounds, with a little more of the whipped ingredient being added a bit at a time. Follow these tips and tricks to keep your baked goods light and fluffy.

HOT TAKE

So, did David and Moira really need to fold in the cheese into their enchilada recipe? Probably not. The cheese sauce didn't really need to be light and fluffy. A mere stirring would suffice in that circumstance. Was this an oversight on the part of the show writers? Maybe...or could it be that Moira's mother's secret recipe was written so that it couldn't be replicated by anyone but her or Adelina? We, the viewers, may never know.

STEP BY STEP

Add the lighter mix to the heavier mix a little at a time. Add a portion of the lighter mix to the heavier mix and use a rubber spatula to cut down to the bottom of the bowl, then drag the spatula toward you. (For example, in the Lock and Key Lime Pie recipe on pg. 174, this would mean adding the whipped cream into the Jell-O mixture.) Be sure to scrape the bottom of the bowl as you go. As you near the edge of the bowl, rotate your wrist to scoop part of the batter up and back on top of itself. You have now completed one fold!

Turn the entire bowl a quarter turn. Repeat by dipping your spatula into the middle of the mix and dragging it to the edge, folding the mixture over itself. Repeat this process until just incorporated. The resulting mixture will be lighter than before. Continue with the next portion of your whipped ingredient.

Once the mixture looks fairly homogeneous, your folding has been successful! Resist the urge to overmix as doing so will remove air from the batter you just worked so hard to retain.

Mozzarella Sticks That
Don't Travel Well, pg. 104

SNACKS,
SIDES, & SAUCES

FOR A QUICK BITE TO TIDE YOU OVER IN BETWEEN MEALS,
THESE DELECTABLE DISHES FIT THE BILL.

JAKE'S MÉNAGE À TROIS THREE-BEAN SALAD

This simple bean salad makes a nice side dish
for your next "party," whether that's for a whiskey or whatever.

INGREDIENTS

- ¼ cup sugar
- ⅔ cup distilled white vinegar
- ⅓ cup vegetable oil
- ½ tsp sea salt
- ½ tsp ground black pepper
- ½ tsp coriander
- ½ tsp celery seed
- 1 (15-oz) can green beans
- 1 lb fresh wax or string beans, chopped
- 1 (15-oz) can kidney beans, drained and rinsed
- 1 white onion, thinly sliced

DIRECTIONS

1. In a large glass bowl, whisk together the sugar, vinegar, oil, salt, pepper, coriander, and celery seed.

2. Add the green beans, wax beans, kidney beans, and onion. Toss well. Marinate overnight before serving.

MAKES 6 SERVINGS

TRIVIA

The town of Schitt's Creek was intentionally depicted as a place free of homophobia in that queer characters exist without criticism of their sexualities. It has been groundbreaking in terms of LGBTQ+ representation.

SOUP IN A BAG

Take it from Twyla: If you're making this earthy mushroom soup to-go,
be sure to double bag it—and don't forget the straw!

INGREDIENTS

- 5 cups sliced fresh mushrooms
- 2 cups chicken broth
- ½ cup chopped onion
- ¼ tsp dried thyme
- 3 Tbsp butter
- 3 Tbsp all-purpose flour
- ½ tsp salt
- ¼ tsp ground black pepper
- 1 cup half-and-half
- 1 Tbsp sherry

DIRECTIONS

1. In a large, heavy saucepan on medium heat, add the mushrooms, broth, onions, and thyme, stirring occasionally until the mushrooms become tender.

2. With an immersion blender, puree the mixture until mushrooms are well minced. Pour the puree into a separate container as you will use the saucepan again to make a roux. If you do not have an immersion blender, use a regular blender.

3. Add the butter to the saucepan and cook for 1 minute.

4. Add in the flour and whisk until the mixture has doubled in size.

5. Add the salt, pepper, half-and-half, and the mushroom puree. Stir constantly and bring soup to a boil briefly, then turn off the heat.

6. Stir in the sherry and serve. Preferably in a bowl.

MAKES 4 SERVINGS

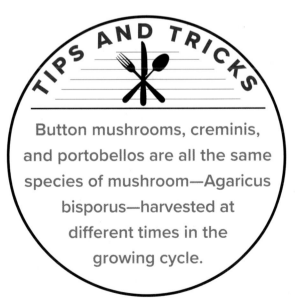

TIPS AND TRICKS

Button mushrooms, creminis, and portobellos are all the same species of mushroom—Agaricus bisporus—harvested at different times in the growing cycle.

HEAVY SALAD THAT'S BASICALLY A CASSEROLE

Though heavy salads are indeed basically casseroles, there's nothing wrong with a casserole now and again.
Packed with autumnal veggies, this hearty salad will keep your mouth occupied should you be forced to have an unprecedentedly uncomfortable lunchtime chin-wag with your mother.

INGREDIENTS
PICKLED ONIONS
- 1 red onion, very thinly sliced
- ½ cup water
- ½ cup distilled white vinegar or apple cider vinegar
- 1½ Tbsp maple syrup
- 1½ tsp sea salt

HEAVY SALAD
- 1½ cups butternut squash, diced
- 1½ cups Brussels sprouts, trimmed and halved
- 1 Tbsp olive oil
- ½ tsp salt
- ½ tsp pepper
- 2¼ cups cooked grain such as brown rice, farro, quinoa, or barley
- ½ cup pomegranate arils
- ⅓ cup toasted pecans
- ⅓ cup crumbled feta cheese
- ½ cup balsamic dressing (see right)
- 2 cups spinach, packed

BALSAMIC DRESSING
- ¼ cup balsamic vinegar
- 1 Tbsp apple cider vinegar
- 2 Tbsp maple syrup
- 1 tsp Dijon mustard
- ¼ tsp salt
- ¼ tsp pepper
- ½ cup extra-virgin olive oil

DIRECTIONS
1. Place the sliced onions in a quart-sized mason jar.

2. In a saucepan over medium heat, combine the water, vinegar, maple syrup, and salt. Bring the mixture to a gentle simmer. Turn off the heat and immediately pour the liquid into the jar. Make sure the onions are completely submerged. Cover and let cool as you begin to roast the vegetables.

3. Preheat the oven to 425 degrees F.

4. Toss the butternut squash and Brussels sprouts with olive oil, salt, and pepper. Place on a baking sheet and roast for 15 minutes. Stir and roast for an additional 5 to 10 minutes or until tender. Set aside to cool.

5. Combine all of the dressing ingredients in a small mason jar and shake well.

6. In a large bowl, combine the cooled grain, roasted vegetables, pomegranate, half the pecans, and half the feta. Toss with ½ cup of dressing. Stir in spinach.

7. Top with pickled onions and remaining pecans and feta. Store any leftover pickled onions in the fridge.

MAKES 6 SERVINGS

CABARET-SE SALAD

Shimmy off that rust and throw together this bedazzled version of a classic caprese salad. The burrata adds an element of pizazz that makes this fit to serve at the Kit Kat.

INGREDIENTS

4–5	heirloom tomatoes, sliced
2	balls fresh burrata cheese
¼	cup fresh basil leaves
2	Tbsp extra-virgin olive oil
	Balsamic vinegar
	Flaky sea salt and freshly ground black pepper

DIRECTIONS

1. Arrange the tomatoes on a platter around the burrata balls. Sprinkle with fresh basil leaves then drizzle with extra-virgin olive oil.
2. Drizzle with balsamic vinegar and season with flaky salt and freshly ground black pepper. Serve at room temperature.

MAKES 4 SERVINGS

TRIVIA

Emily Hampshire (Stevie Budd) used to tell people her dream acting role was to play Sally Bowles in *Cabaret*. She was ecstatic to finally get that chance in season 5, episode 14 ("Life Is a Cabaret") when Stevie portrays Sally in a local production of the classic musical.

HAPPY ENDING MASSAGED KALE SALAD

You don't have to pay extra for this happy ending,
but be sure to really spend a few minutes massaging the olive oil
into the kale leaves for a truly blissful salad experience.

INGREDIENTS
DRESSING

- 6 Tbsp extra-virgin olive oil
- 1½ Tbsp orange juice
- 1½ Tbsp balsamic vinegar
- 1½ Tbsp maple syrup
- ½ tsp salt
- ½ tsp freshly ground black pepper
- Zest of 1 orange

SALAD

- 10 oz kale, destemmed and chopped
- 1 tsp olive oil
- 2 oranges
- ⅓ cup pistachios, chopped
- 4 oz crumbled chèvre

DIRECTIONS

1. In a mason jar, combine all of the dressing ingredients and shake vigorously. Set aside.
2. Place kale in a large salad bowl and drizzle olive oil and the juice of half the orange you zested for the dressing. Using your hands, massage the kale for 2 to 3 minutes.
3. Using a sharp knife, peel the remaining 2 oranges, removing as much of the white pith as possible. Slice the oranges into segments.
4. Pour the dressing over the salad and toss to combine. Top with the oranges, pistachios, and chèvre. Pairs nicely with the Big Piece of Fish on pg. 80.

MAKES 4 SERVINGS

TRIVIA

The series finale ("Happy Ending") was not Dan Levy's first time acting in a wedding scene. At the start of his career, he played an extra in the music video for Kelly Clarkson's "Behind These Hazel Eyes." In the scene, Kelly is a disgruntled bride who runs out of her wedding, and Levy appears ever-so-briefly as one of her wedding guests.

MALL PRETZELS WITH SHAME SAUCE

Do not feel shame about the mall pretzels (even if you ate more of them than you're willing to admit after that one breakup). You may need to bake in several rounds if they do not fit on your baking sheets. No shame in that either.

INGREDIENTS

PRETZELS

- 1 (.25-oz) package active dry yeast
- 2 Tbsp brown sugar
- 1⅛ tsp salt
- 3½ cups warm water (110 degrees F), divided
- 3 cups all-purpose flour
- 1 cup bread flour
- 2 Tbsp baking soda
- 2 Tbsp butter, melted
- 2 Tbsp coarse kosher salt

SHAME SAUCE

- ¼ cup honey
- ½ cup mayonnaise
- 2 Tbsp yellow mustard
- ¼ cup barbecue sauce (we recommend Budd's Bourbon BBQ Sauce, pg. 114)
- 1 Tbsp lemon juice

DIRECTIONS

1. In the bowl of a stand mixer, dissolve the yeast, brown sugar, and salt in 1½ cups warm water.
2. Add both flours to the mixture and knead using a stand mixer fitted with a dough hook until the dough is elastic and smooth. If kneading by hand, knead the dough on a floured surface for about 8 minutes.
3. Place in a greased bowl, then turn the dough to lightly coat the surface. Cover and let the dough rise in a warm area for 1 hour.
4. Meanwhile, mix the remaining 2 cups of warm water and baking soda in a wide, shallow plastic container or baking dish. This container will be used to dip the pretzels in, so the wider it is, the easier dipping will be.
5. Preheat the oven to 450 degrees F and

TIPS AND TRICKS

Dipping the pretzels in baking soda is what gives them their glossy brown exterior. Sodium hydroxide (lye) also works in a pinch, but is not as delicious!

lightly grease two baking sheets.

6. Divide the risen dough into 12 pieces. Roll each piece into a ball and then into a long, thin rope. Twist into a pretzel shape and dip into the baking soda solution. Transfer to a paper towel briefly to absorb excess moisture, then quickly flip onto a greased baking sheet. Let rise for 15 to 20 minutes.

7. Bake the pretzels until golden brown, about 8 to 10 minutes.

8. Meanwhile, in a mixing bowl, whisk together all sauce ingredients.

9. Remove the pretzels from the oven. Brush them with melted butter and sprinkle with coarse salt. Serve warm with the sauce and feel no remorse as you dig in.

MAKES 12 MALL PRETZELS

MOZZARELLA STICKS THAT DON'T TRAVEL WELL

I should warn you, they've already lost a lot of their shape.
At least there's no freezer burn when you make them from scratch!

INGREDIENTS

2 eggs, beaten

¼ cup water

1½ cups Italian seasoned breadcrumbs

½ tsp garlic salt

⅔ cup all-purpose flour

⅓ cup cornstarch

1 quart canola oil for deep frying

1 (16-oz) package mozzarella cheese sticks

DIRECTIONS

1. In a small bowl, mix the eggs and water and set aside.

2. In a medium bowl, combine the breadcrumbs and garlic salt. In a second medium bowl, combine the flour and cornstarch. In a large, heavy saucepan on medium, heat the oil to 365 degrees F.

3. Working one by one, coat each mozzarella stick in the flour mixture, the egg mixture, and, finally, the breadcrumbs.

4. Fry the mozzarella sticks until golden brown, about 30 seconds. Remove and drain on a paper towel-lined plate.

5. Eat immediately, exactly where you are. Do not even walk across the room. These do not travel well.

MAKES 8 SERVINGS

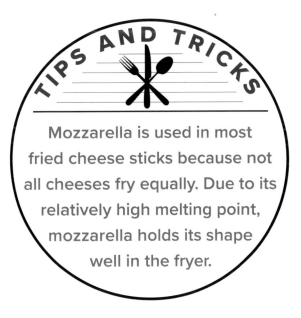

TIPS AND TRICKS

Mozzarella is used in most fried cheese sticks because not all cheeses fry equally. Due to its relatively high melting point, mozzarella holds its shape well in the fryer.

APOTHECARY APPLESAUCE

Organic applesauce? Who are you, Gwyneth Paltrow?
This tangy applesauce is so good you'll forget you even had a bébé to feed
it to in the first place. On the bright side, if you end up finishing it off
yourself, you can always feed the bébé some granola bars, right?

INGREDIENTS

1½ cups apple cider
 1 lb Honeycrisp (or similar) apples,
    peeled, cored, and chopped
 1 tsp cinnamon
 1 tsp lemon juice
    Pinch of sea salt

DIRECTIONS

1. In a medium saucepan over medium heat, bring the apple cider to a boil, stirring occasionally. Cook until you are left with 1 cup of concentrated apple cider, about 20 to 25 minutes.
2. Add apples to the cider and return the mixture to a boil. Reduce the heat to medium-low and cover. Cook until the apples are very soft, about 15 minutes.
3. Add the remaining ingredients. Cook over medium-low heat until the apples are broken up and most of the liquid has evaporated, about 5 minutes.
4. For chunky applesauce, mash the mixture with the back of a wooden spoon until it has reached your desired consistency. For applesauce as smooth as a bébé's bottom, let the mixture cool before pulsing in a food processor until creamy.

**MAKES ENOUGH FOR 1 HUNGRY BÉBÉ
(APPROXIMATELY 1½ CUPS)**

TRIVIA

Apothecary is a mostly archaic term that refers to a shop where medicines were made and sold. Medieval cure-alls might have included herbs and minerals, perhaps ingredients that would have appeared in David and Patrick's shop. However, such concoctions would have also included animal meat, fat, and skin; human saliva; and earwax.
Ew, indeed.

POKER NIGHT MEATBALLS

Talk about having an ace up your sleeve. Serve these savory bites with stir-fried veggies while accusing your friend of being a cheater.

INGREDIENTS
MEATBALLS
- 16 oz lean ground turkey
- ½ cup panko breadcrumbs
- ¼ cup finely chopped green onion
- 1 large egg
- 1 tsp freshly grated ginger
  or ¼ tsp ground ginger
- 1 garlic clove, minced
- 2 tsp sesame oil

TERIYAKI SAUCE
- ¼ cup light brown sugar, lightly packed
- 2 Tbsp hoisin sauce
- 1 Tbsp soy sauce
- ½ Tbsp sesame oil
- 1 medium garlic clove, minced
- ½ tsp fresh ginger or ⅛ tsp ground ginger

DIRECTIONS
1. Preheat the oven to 400 degrees F. Line a rimmed baking sheet with foil.
2. In a large bowl, mix all meatball ingredients together until just combined.
3. Roll the mixture into 1¼- to 1½-inch meatballs.
4. Bake for 10 to 12 minutes or until juices run clear or the internal temperature reaches 165 degrees F.

5. In a small saucepan on medium-low heat, combine all teriyaki sauce ingredients. Simmer while stirring frequently until the sauce has slightly thickened, about 2 to 4 minutes.
6. Transfer the warm meatballs to a large mixing bowl. Pour the sauce over them and toss to combine.

MAKES 5 SERVINGS

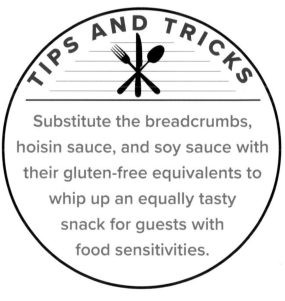

TIPS AND TRICKS

Substitute the breadcrumbs, hoisin sauce, and soy sauce with their gluten-free equivalents to whip up an equally tasty snack for guests with food sensitivities.

TED'S VETERINARY CLINIC DOG TREATS
(ALSO FOR HUMANS)

When the bunny cam is turned off for good, try giving out homemade dog treats! While not as sexy as Dr. Miguel's marketing, these homemade dog treats can be given out to your patients to guarantee their return business. These healthy dog treats are as safe for Fido as they are for David.

INGREDIENTS

- 5 cups whole wheat flour
- 4 eggs
- 1 (15 oz) can pumpkin
- Heaping ¼ cup peanut butter
- 1 tsp salt
- 1 tsp ground cinnamon

DIRECTIONS

1. Preheat the oven to 350 degrees F.
2. In a stand mixer, combine all ingredients and blend until just combined. If the dough is too dry, add 1 Tbsp of water at a time until it is workable.
3. Divide the dough into four pieces.
4. Roll each piece into a long rope about ½- to 1-inch in diameter.
5. Using a sharp knife, cut pieces ½- to 1-inch wide.
6. Place the pieces on a parchment-lined baking sheet and bake for 30 to 35 minutes, or freeze to save for game night. Once cooked, these can be stored in the fridge for up to 2 weeks.

MAKES ENOUGH FOR THE WHOLE CLINIC (ROUGHLY 100 TREATS)

TRIVIA

Actor and writer Dan Levy (David) is a big proponent of rescuing animals. He rescued his late dog Redmond, a dachshund-corgi mix who was his loyal companion for 10 years.

PINE CONE PESTO

You don't need to go on a journey to harvest pine cones for this tasty sauce. Pairs well with fresh pasta or chicken. Round out the meal with pine cone wine.

INGREDIENTS

- 3 cups chopped fresh basil
- 1 cup extra-virgin olive oil
- ½ cup pine nuts
- ⅔ cup grated Parmesan cheese
- 2 Tbsp minced garlic
- ½ tsp chili powder
- ½ tsp sea salt

DIRECTIONS

1. Place the basil in a food processor or blender. Pour in about 1 Tbsp of the oil and blend into a paste.

2. While the food processor is running, slowly add remaining oil and the remaining ingredients.

3. Continue to blend until smooth. Serve fresh or freeze until needed.

MAKES ABOUT 2 CUPS

TIPS AND TRICKS

Traditionally, this sauce is made with a large mortar and pestle. The word pesto comes from the Italian word "pestare," meaning "to crush" or "to pound."

BUDD'S BOURBON BBQ SAUCE

Just like Nana Budd used to make.
Spiked with whiskey, this BBQ sauce pairs
well with...well, more whiskey.

INGREDIENTS

½ onion, minced
6 cloves garlic, minced
¾ cup bourbon whiskey
½ tsp ground black pepper
½ Tbsp salt
2 cups ketchup
¼ cup tomato paste
⅓ cup cider vinegar
1 Tbsp plus 1 tsp liquid smoke
¼ cup Worcestershire sauce
½ cup packed brown sugar
½ tsp hot sauce

DIRECTIONS

1. In a skillet over medium heat, combine the onion, garlic, and whiskey. Simmer for about 8 minutes or until the onion is translucent.
2. Add the remaining ingredients. Cover and bring to a boil. Reduce the heat to low and simmer while stirring occasionally for 20 minutes.
3. If not using the sauce immediately, store it in an airtight container in the fridge for up to a week. The flavor will deepen after a day or two in the fridge.

MAKES 2½ CUPS

TIPS AND TRICKS

Since alcohol is not usually fully evaporated in recipes with shorter cook times (as opposed to hours of simmering), don't share this boozy sauce with the bébés.

Turkish St. Nicholas,
pg. 138

DRINKS

WHETHER YOU'RE LOOKING FOR A SMOOTHIE OR SOMETHING STRONGER, YOUR LIQUID RESPITE IS JUST A SIP AWAY.

TWYLA'S MEADOW HARVEST SMOOTHIE

Meadow Harvest is exactly how it sounds in that it changes every day. It's fruity at times, and other times it's not. Today's Meadow Harvest Smoothie calls for ingredients you may have around your kitchen. Or maybe not. Just depends!

INGREDIENTS

- 1 frozen banana, cut into chunks
- 1 cup seedless grapes
- 6 oz non-dairy vanilla yogurt
- ½ apple, cored and chopped
- 1½ cups packed fresh spinach leaves
- ¼ cup oat milk, plus more as needed

DIRECTIONS

1. Add the ingredients to the blender. Cover and blend until smooth. Scrape down sides as needed. Add additional oat milk to thin if needed.

2. Pour into glass and serve. I'll have one if you're making one.

MAKES 1 SERVING

TIPS AND TRICKS

When crafting a smoothie to suit your taste, follow this formula: 2–3 parts fruit and/or vegetables, 1–1½ parts liquid, and ½ part yogurt or other thickener.

NEW JOB CHAMPAGNE TOAST

Just drop a little raisin in there. It might not revive the bubbles, but who doesn't love a champagne-soaked raisin to finish off a celebratory toast?

INGREDIENTS
½ bottle of champagne (flat, if you're a purist)
2 raisins, preferably Sun-Maid

DIRECTIONS
1. Pour the champagne into two flutes. Drop a raisin into each to "revive the bubbles."
2. Make a toast.
3. Fish out the raisin with your finger and enjoy. (Optional: Eat the champagne-soaked raisin and question every decision you have made that has led you to this point in your life.)

MAKES 2 SERVINGS

TIPS AND TRICKS

You're asking a lot of that raisin. According to the test kitchen at *Cook's Illustrated*, the best way to use flat champagne is to treat it like a cooking wine.

GALAPAGOS RESEARCH RUM PUNCH

This batch cocktail is perfect to share with
your fellow researchers as you bond over the new species
you've just discovered in the Galapagos Islands.

INGREDIENTS

½ cup fresh lime juice
1 cup simple syrup
1½ cups amber rum
2 cups orange juice
4–5 dashes bitters
Freshly grated nutmeg

GARNISH

Orange wedges

DIRECTIONS

1. Add the lime juice, simple syrup, rum, and orange juice to a pitcher. Add the bitters and grated nutmeg to taste. Refrigerate for at least 2 hours while you continue your Galapagos research.
2. Serve chilled over ice and garnish with orange wedges.

MAKES 6 SERVINGS

TRIVIA

When Alexis is Skyping with Ted while he is in the Galapagos Islands, the two actors were in the same room. Annie Murphy and Dustin Milligan filmed all of Alexis and Ted's Skype sessions together.

HERB ERTLINGER'S WINE SPRITZER WITH RADISH

The radish is just for looks here, but wouldn't strawberry radish wine be refreshing? Just don't let this one oxidize or you might not recognize the taste.

●◆●

INGREDIENTS

1 cup chilled fruit wine of choice
½ cup chilled club soda or La Croix
1 radish

DIRECTIONS

1. With a sharp paring knife, slice the radish into rounds. Take a round and slice halfway through the radish from the center to the outer edge so that it may be used to garnish the rim of your wine glass.
2. Pour the wine into glasses and top with club soda or La Croix. Garnish with a radish slice.

MAKES 2 SERVINGS

TIPS AND TRICKS

Radishes reportedly don't make for good sipping, but fruit wine is commonly made from berries (e.g., elderberries), plums, pomegranates, and more.

ROSÉ SANGRIA

We like this one for the wine and not the label.
Does that make sense?

INGREDIENTS

1 bottle rosé wine
½ cup vodka
1 cup pineapple juice
¼ cup triple sec
½ cup simple syrup
1 orange, sliced into rounds
1 lemon, sliced into rounds
6 oz fresh raspberries

DIRECTIONS

1. Add the wine, vodka, pineapple juice, triple sec, and simple syrup to a pitcher. Refrigerate until chilled, about 1 hour.

2. Stir citrus and raspberries into the chilled sangria at least 30 minutes before serving over ice.

MAKES 6 SERVINGS

TRIVIA

According to Dan Levy, a fan of the show told him they came out to their family using the show's metaphor of "into the wine, not the label."

DAVID'S MACCHIATO

Is it pretentious and oddly specific?
Yes. But after the first sip, it may become your go-to as well.

INGREDIENTS

8 oz skim milk
2 tsp sugar or 1 Tbsp vanilla syrup
1–2 shots of espresso

GARNISH

Caramel sauce
Cocoa powder

DIRECTIONS

1. Using either the stovetop or microwave, heat the milk until it is hot but not scalding.
2. Froth the milk. If you don't have a milk frother, place the hot milk in a large blender and pulse several times until foam forms.
3. Pour the sugar into the bottom of a mug. Add the frothed milk.
4. Pull the shot(s) of espresso, then add to the mug.
5. Garnish with a drizzle of caramel sauce and a sprinkle of cocoa powder.

MAKES 1 SERVING

TRIVIA

Wardrobe was a critical element of storytelling. Dan Levy spent hours searching online for the perfect designer pieces with which to dress the Roses. Outfitting the main cast in bespoke duds was an intentional choice, an homage to the wealth and circumstance of the world the Roses came from and a stark contrast to their lives in Schitt's Creek.

A LITTLE BIT ALEXIS LATTE

A little bit of coffee, when you first wake up.
A little bit of steamed milk, poured in your cup.
A little bit of la la la la la la la—a little bit of latte!

INGREDIENTS

- 8 oz milk
- 1–2 shots of espresso
- 1 Tbsp vanilla syrup

DIRECTIONS

1. Using either the stovetop or microwave, heat the milk until it is hot but not scalding.
2. Froth the milk. If you don't have a milk frother, place the hot milk in a large blender and pulse several times until foam forms.
3. Pull the shot(s) of espresso, then add to the mug. Stir in the vanilla syrup.
4. Slowly pour in the frothed milk.

MAKES 1 SERVING

TRIVIA

Annie Murphy was given creative liberties on the song "A Little Bit Alexis." She took it very seriously and worked with her husband (Menno Versteeg, a Canadian musician) and a friend to create the pop-y, parody earworm that Alexis performs to audition for *Cabaret*.

BARN PUNCH

Definitely better than room temperature vodka.
Just don't use those well water ice cubes!

INGREDIENTS

1 (32-oz) bottle cranberry juice

1 (12-oz) can apple juice concentrate

1 cup orange juice

4 cups ice

1 (750-mL) bottle of champagne or 1 (1-L)
   bottle of ginger ale

GARNISH

1 apple, sliced

DIRECTIONS

1. In a glass drink dispenser, combine the
cranberry juice, apple juice concentrate, orange
juice, and ice.

2. Stir until combined, then slowly pour
in the champagne. For a non-alcoholic version,
substitute the champagne for a 1-liter
bottle of ginger ale. Top with sliced apples
before serving.

MAKES 10 SERVINGS

TRIVIA

Many fans consider the finale
of Season 2 ("Happy
Anniversary") to be a turning
point for the Rose family.
Throughout the episode,
the four Roses can be seen
accepting their circumstances
and embracing their life
in Schitt's Creek.

SURPRISE ME SMOOTHIE

Oats give this smoothie a nice hearty texture and dose of fiber
that make it the perfect post-run pick-me-up.

INGREDIENTS

⅓ cup rolled oats

⅓ cup Greek yogurt

⅓ cup frozen raspberries

1 frozen banana, chopped

½ cup milk

DIRECTIONS

Place all ingredients in a blender and blend
until well combined. For a thinner smoothie,
add more milk.

MAKES 1 SERVING

Pack even more vitamins
into your smoothie by tossing
in a handful of spinach, or amp
up the creaminess by adding
half an avocado for
a rich finish.

PRECIOUS LOVE

This cocktail may not teach you to be a better man,
but it will have you begging for more. Thawed frozen strawberries
can be substituted for fresh in a pinch.

INGREDIENTS

2 large fresh strawberries, sliced
½ oz lemon juice
½ oz maple syrup
2 oz bourbon
1 splash club soda

GARNISH

1 strawberry

DIRECTIONS

1. In a cocktail shaker, add sliced strawberries, lemon juice, and maple syrup. Muddle until the strawberries are mashed. Add the bourbon and stir.
2. Fill a Collins glass with ice and pour the mixture over the top.
3. Add a splash of club soda, give it a gentle stir, and garnish with a strawberry.

MAKES 1 SERVING

TRIVIA

Dan Levy specifically wrote scenes where Moira is drunk into the show because he thought Catherine O'Hara was exceptionally good at playing inebriated characters.

TURKISH ST. NICHOLAS

This aromatic cocktail is the best gift Turkish St. Nicholas could give.

INGREDIENTS

TEA SYRUP

2 oz loose leaf black tea

¾ cup water

¾ cup white sugar

COCKTAIL

2 oz vodka

¾ oz fresh lemon juice

¾ oz tea syrup

2 dashes orange bitters

Spritz of orange blossom water

DIRECTIONS

1. Steep the tea in hot water for 5 minutes in a small saucepan. Strain the tea leaves.

2. Add the sugar and bring the liquid to a simmer. Stir until the sugar has dissolved completely. Can be stored in an airtight container for up to 3 days.

3. Combine vodka, lemon juice, tea syrup, and bitters in a shaker and add ice. Shake and strain into a chilled coupe glass.

4. Using an atomizer, mist the finished cocktail with orange blossom water.

SERVES 1

TIPS AND TRICKS

Don't have an atomizer? Add about 1 tsp of the suggested liquid into the glass to coat its interior, then pour it out. Your glass is now "rinsed" and ready.

SUNRISE BAY

You needn't be the head of surgery nor a soap opera starlet to enjoy this fruity cocktail.

INGREDIENTS

1 oz vodka

1 oz peach schnapps

2 oz cranberry juice

2 oz orange juice

½ oz lime juice

GARNISH

Orange wedge

DIRECTIONS

1. Shake the vodka, peach schnapps, cranberry juice, orange juice, and lime juice in a cocktail shaker with ice.

2. Strain the drink into an ice-filled rocks glass. Garnish with the orange wedge. You can worry about the centuries-old curse that plagues this wretched town later; now is not the time for pettifogging.

MAKES 1 SERVING

> ### TRIVIA
>
> In addition to starring in *Sunrise Bay*, Moira Rose was an accomplished actress of stage and screen. Her résumé also includes voiceovers, commercial work, and even a gig as a hand model.

HAIR OF THE MUTT

This drink feels warm and cozy, like a long hug or a flattering beard.

INGREDIENTS

2 oz bourbon
½ oz maple syrup
1 oz cream
  Ice

GARNISH

Nutmeg

DIRECTIONS

1. Add the bourbon and maple syrup to a cocktail shaker. Stir until fully dissolved, then add the cream and ice.

2. Shake and strain the drink into a coupe glass. Garnish with a sprinkle of nutmeg. Wait, are you crying?

MAKES 1 SERVING

TRIVIA

Many of the Canadian actors on the series have also appeared in Canada's long-running teen drama *Degrassi*, including Tim Rozon (Mutt), Noah Reid (Patrick), Jennifer Robertson (Jocelyn), and Dan Levy (David).

APOTHECARY ROBBER'S PICNIC

IN "LOVE LETTERS" (season 5, episode 2), Stevie and David are in the Apothecary when a balaclava-clad gentleman enters the scene. Following a brief, distressing exchange in which a weapon definitely could have been present, they proceed to load up two totes of product and send the criminal on his merry way. While there was no explicit mention of a picnic in the episode, the items chosen by the victims of the harrowing holdup could serve as a perfect springtime picnic lunch.

PLANNING

While we can't endorse pillaging the shelves of your local mercantile prior to your lunchtime rendezvous, the following tips will ensure you pick just the right items.

● When choosing the best foods for a picnic, there are a few things to consider. Your selections should be portable, safe to eat without requiring heat or refrigeration, and should err on the neater side to limit the amount of cleanup required.

● Depending on the ingredients, leftovers may not be safe to eat after an afternoon in the sun, so take care to pack only as much food as needed. After all, this isn't some all-one-can-consume smörgåsbord.

● For your "booze in a bag," skip the red or white wine and opt for a chilled Syrah rosé. Its full-bodied flavors pair well with an aged cheddar. A fruity, dry rosé pairs well with a soft, creamy brie. But as Stevie says, "Cheese goes good with wine," so just pick your favorites. Serve some crudite—like miniature bell peppers and baby carrots—alongside your cheese to balance your snacking.

● Pasta and bean salad are perfect picks as

they can be as light or as hearty as you choose.

- Handheld breads that don't require fussy cutting, like focaccia, pretzels, or naan, can be served with a variety of dips, like tapenade, hummus, or tzatziki. Sandwiches are of course a classic, but don't discount other handhelds like empanadas or burritos. And, of course, you mustn't forget dessert. Cookies and dessert bars work best and can be easily stacked in plastic containers without too much fuss.

OUR PERSONAL *TASTES LIKE SCHITT* PICNIC PICKS:

- Jake's Ménage à Trois Three-Bean Salad (pg. 92)
- Bus Ride Brownies (pg. 162)
- Mall Pretzels With Shame Sauce (pg. 102)

PACKING

While a cloth tote like the one David handed the robber makes for a convenient receptacle for stolen goods, we don't recommend it for packing your picnic, lest your frangible items find themselves utterly ruined in transport. Packing your picnic in a flat-bottomed insulated bag will allow you to keep your items organized, cool, and veritably un-smushed. Place a flat ice pack and your cold beverages on the bottom layer, followed by your meal. This ensures your food and beverages will be most effectively chilled. On top of your edible fare, pack lightweight plates, utensils, napkins, and a flexible plastic cutting board. Packing these items on top allows for efficiency when unpacking, as you can place food items directly on your cutting board for ease of serving.

PICNICKING

While you may not be able to drive all the way to Elm Valley and picnic among the cherry blossoms (season 5, episode 4) or lunch on top of a mountain after a long hike and simultaneously ruin a proposal (season 5, episode 13), you can find a perfectly good picnic spot in your local parks, forests, on the shore of a lake or river, or even on the lawns of public places like universities or museums. Wherever you choose, don't forget to pack a plastic bag for easy cleanup so you can be sure not to leave trash behind.

Though the type of skincare serums the robber got away with were never specified, the most important one you'll need for your picnic is sunscreen. Choose one with an SPF of at least 30, and reapply it throughout your afternoon of snacking and schmoozing. Stashing your sunscreen in your cooler bag is a great way of ensuring that it does not overheat and lose its effectiveness.

Depending on your local weather and season, consider bringing a light jacket, or if it's your color, perhaps a poly-blend hooded sweatshirt in aubergine?

DESSERTS

AND NOW FOR THE GRAND FINALE: DECADENT DELIGHTS CERTAIN TO BE THE HAPPY ENDING OF ANY MEAL.

Sex in a Pan, pg. 166

RONNIE'S RED CARPET COOKIES

You're going to have to settle for the 20-foot merlot carpet from my garage or these cookies. Take your pick. This recipe makes enough for all of your most esteemed guests.

INGREDIENTS

- 6 Tbsp butter
- 1 cup confectioners' sugar
- 1 tsp cornstarch
- 1 (18.25-oz) box red velvet cake mix
- 2 large eggs
- 1 tsp lemon zest

DIRECTIONS

1. Preheat the oven to 375 degrees F.

2. In a microwave-safe bowl, melt the butter and set aside to cool.

3. Mix the sugar and cornstarch together in a shallow dish. Place cake mix, melted butter, eggs, and lemon zest in a large mixing bowl, then mix by hand with a rubber spatula until a dough forms, about 2 to 3 minutes.

4. Using a small cookie scoop or spoon, shape the dough into 1-inch balls. Roll each ball in the sugar mixture and place on ungreased baking sheets about 2 inches apart.

5. Bake on the center rack of the oven for 9 to 10 minutes or until just set.

6. Transfer to a wire rack to cool before serving.

MAKES 24 COOKIES

TRIVIA

Karen Robinson said one of the reasons she was interested in playing Ronnie was because of how low-maintenance she is in terms of makeup and wardrobe.

PATRICK'S SIMPLY THE BEST CHOCOLATE PUDDING

If you're looking for a pudding that's better than all the rest, this one is rich, chocolaty, and meant to be. It's like an incredible cover of a classic you already loved: simply the best.

INGREDIENTS

½ cup white sugar
3 Tbsp unsweetened cocoa powder
¼ cup cornstarch
⅛ tsp salt
2¾ cups milk
2 Tbsp butter, room temperature
1 tsp vanilla extract

DIRECTIONS

1. In a heavy-bottomed saucepan, combine the sugar, cocoa powder, cornstarch, and salt. Whisk in the milk and bring the mixture to a boil over medium. Stir constantly until the pudding is thick enough to coat the back of a metal spoon, about 2 to 3 minutes.

2. Remove from heat, and stir in butter and vanilla. Let cool briefly. Spoon into small glass dessert cups and serve warm or chill in the refrigerator until serving.

MAKES 4 SERVINGS

TRIVIA

Noah Reid created his own arrangement for "The Best": he took Tina Turner's 1989 song (which itself was a cover of Bonnie Tyler's 1988 song) and made it slow, sweet, and completely heartfelt. The track hit #1 on the Canadian iTunes Soundtrack chart.

FARM WITCHES PEANUT BUTTER THINGS

Are they peanut butter bars? Peanut butter squares, maybe? Whatever you call them, you're going to want to circle back for these peanut butter bites; just be careful not to fill up if you're planning on spending your afternoon eating cheese.

INGREDIENTS

1½ cups butter, divided

4 cups confectioners' sugar

2 cups conventional peanut butter (natural peanut butter will not work as well)

2 cups graham cracker crumbs

1½ cups semisweet chocolate chips

GARNISH

Flaky sea salt (Maldon works well)

DIRECTIONS

1. Grease an 11-by-13-inch baking dish.

2. In a medium saucepan, melt 1 cup of butter. Remove from the heat. Stir in the sugar and peanut butter. When fully incorporated, stir in the graham cracker crumbs.

3. Pour the mixture into the baking dish to form the crust and press it down evenly with your hands or a rubber spatula.

4. Meanwhile, as the crust sets, in a microwave-safe bowl, melt the remaining ½ cup butter and chocolate chips in 30-second intervals, stirring between each interval until melted.

5. Pour the chocolate mixture over the crust and spread it in an even layer.

6. Refrigerate for at least an hour before slicing into small squares. Garnish with a sprinkle of sea salt flakes before serving.

MAKES 64 SERVINGS

TIPS AND TRICKS

While the sprinkling of flaky sea salt is not entirely necessary, this topping plays off the salt in the peanut butter for a well-balanced finish.

BOOZY EGGNOG MILKSHAKE

"Ew, there's no booze in that!" is what you would say
if you didn't add a shot or two of rum, whiskey, or cognac
to make this Christmas milkshake a little more Moira.

INGREDIENTS

  2 cups vanilla ice cream

  ¾ cup eggnog

  ½ tsp nutmeg

  ½ tsp cinnamon

1–2 shots of dark rum, whiskey, or cognac

DIRECTIONS

1. In a blender, blend all ingredients until smooth.

2. Pour into two glasses and top with a sprinkle of cinnamon. Garnish with a cinnamon stick or two before serving.

MAKES 2 SERVINGS

TIPS AND TRICKS

Hoping to become a bit more ebrious at your next holiday soiree? Add more hooch: try ¼ oz of ginger cordial or peppermint schnapps.

FOUR MONTH-IVERSARY BIG COOKIE

The perfect way to celebrate the longest relationship you've ever had, even if it's only four months. You can keep this big cookie all to yourself or serve it after a course of charred meat at the family barbecue.

INGREDIENTS

2¼ cups all-purpose flour
1 tsp baking soda
1 tsp salt
1 cup (2 sticks) butter, softened
¾ cup granulated sugar
¾ cup packed brown sugar
1 tsp vanilla extract
2 eggs
2 cups semi-sweet chocolate chips

DIRECTIONS

1. Preheat the oven to 375 degrees F. Grease a medium-sized heart-shaped baking pan.
2. In a medium bowl, combine the flour, baking soda, and salt. In a stand mixer or with a hand mixer, cream the butter, granulated sugar, brown sugar, and vanilla extract.
3. In the stand mixer bowl, add the eggs one at a time, beating after each addition. Scrape down the sides of the bowl and beat until combined. Gradually beat in flour mixture until just combined. Once the dough has a consistent texture, fold in the chocolate chips using a rubber spatula.
4. Press a thin layer of cookie dough into the prepared pan. The dough should be no more than ½ inch thick.

5. Bake until golden brown, about 15 to 18 minutes. If the pan is large, it may need additional time. Let cool in the pan before serving.

MAKES 2 BIG COOKIES

TRIVIA

Noah Reid, the actor who plays Patrick, has been acting professionally since he was a child. From 1997 to 2004, he voiced the titular turtle on the children's cartoon show *Franklin*.

JOCELYN'S NANAIMO BARS

This recipe makes plenty, so don't accidentally double it.
Roland is on diabetes watch, after all.

INGREDIENTS

LAYER 1

½ cup butter, softened

¼ cup sugar

5 Tbsp unsweetened cocoa powder

1 egg

1¾ cups graham cracker crumbs

1 cup unsweetened shredded coconut

½ cup finely chopped almonds, optional

LAYER 2

½ cup butter, softened

3 Tbsp heavy cream

2 Tbsp powdered instant vanilla pudding mix

2 cups confectioners' sugar

LAYER 3

4 (1-oz) squares semisweet baking chocolate

2 tsp butter

DIRECTIONS

1. In a double boiler, add ½ cup butter and stir until melted. Add the sugar and cocoa powder and continue to stir until the mixture is smooth. Quickly beat in the egg, stirring until thick, 2 to 3 minutes.

2. Remove from heat and stir in the graham cracker crumbs, coconut, and almonds if using. Mix until the graham cracker crumbs are fully incorporated. The mixture should be dry and crumbly. Press into the bottom of a greased 8-by-8-inch pan lined with parchment paper. Refrigerate as you make the next layer.

3. For the second layer, in the bowl of a stand mixer, cream together ½ cup butter, heavy cream, and the pudding mix until light and fluffy. Scrape down the sides as needed. Slowly add sugar and continue to beat for 1 minute.

4. Using an offset spatula, spread the mixture over the bottom layer in the pan. Return to the refrigerator until needed.

5. In a medium bowl, microwave the chocolate and 2 tsp of butter together in 30-second intervals. Once the chocolate is melted, work quickly to spread evenly as the final layer.

6. Refrigerate for at least 1 hour. Use a sharp knife to cut into squares before serving.

MAKES 16 SERVINGS

A truly Canadian confection, Nanaimo bars were invented in the Great White North and named after the British Columbia city of Nanaimo.

BUS RIDE BROWNIES

They may not be quite as exciting as Jocelyn's, but they are fudgy and delicious. Pair these brownies with oxygen drops, antibacterial wipes, and military-grade caffeine pills for a naughty night of debauchery.

INGREDIENTS

- ½ cup butter
- 1 cup white sugar
- 2 eggs
- 1 tsp vanilla extract
- ⅓ cup unsweetened cocoa powder
- ½ cup all-purpose flour
- ¼ tsp salt
- ¼ tsp baking powder

DIRECTIONS

1. Preheat the oven to 350 degrees F. Grease and flour an 8-by-8-inch pan.

2. In a microwaveable mug, heat the butter for 30 seconds or until melted. Pour into a large mixing bowl and stir in sugar, eggs, and vanilla.

3. Gently stir in the cocoa, flour, salt, and baking powder. Mix until well incorporated, but do not overmix. Spread the batter into the prepared pan.

4. Bake for 25 to 30 minutes. Let cool before cutting. Store in plastic storage container to keep fresh for the ride to the concert (or casino, if the former gets canceled).

MAKES 16 SERVINGS

TIPS AND TRICKS

Modern pot brownies can be traced back to a recipe for Hashish Fudge in *The Alice B. Toklas Cook Book*, first published in 1954.

HAPPY DAY CAKE

You don't have to be "Alex" and "Davis" (sorry, David) to enjoy this cake on your happy day. This yellow cake is best eaten last minute at a celebration you definitely did not forget.

INGREDIENTS

- 1 cup butter, room temperature
- 2 cups white sugar
- 4 eggs, separated, room temperature
- 1 tsp vanilla extract
- 1 Tbsp baking powder
- ½ tsp salt plus a pinch
- 3 cups all-purpose flour
- 1 cup milk, room temperature

HAPPY DAY BUTTERCREAM

- 2 sticks unsalted butter, softened
- 1 pound sifted confectioners' sugar
- 1½ tsp vanilla extract
- 2 Tbsp milk

DIRECTIONS

1. Preheat the oven to 350 degrees F. Grease and flour a 9-by-13-inch pan.

2. In a stand mixer or with a hand mixer, cream the butter and sugar together until fluffy, about 5 minutes. Add the egg yolks one at a time, thoroughly combining before adding the next one. Mix in the vanilla extract.

3. Sift together the baking powder, salt, and flour. Add the flour mixture to the butter mixture in three batches, alternating with the milk. Mix after each addition. Scrape down the sides and bottom of the bowl and beat for 60 more seconds.

4. In a separate bowl, beat the egg whites with the pinch of salt until soft peaks form, about 1 minute. Fold one-third of the egg whites into the cake batter to lighten it, then gently fold in the remaining egg whites. Pour the batter into the prepared pan.

5. Bake until a toothpick inserted into the center comes out clean, about 35 minutes. Cool completely.

6. Meanwhile, cream the butter until smooth and fluffy. Gradually beat in the sugar until fully incorporated.

7. Beat in the vanilla extract, then pour in the milk and beat for an additional 3 to 4 minutes. Frost your Happy Day Cake to celebrate all of your children.

MAKES 16 SERVINGS

SEX IN A PAN

We can all have some Sex in a Pan, and then we'll have dessert!
Is it just me, or is it this dessert that's making me horny?

INGREDIENTS

- 1 (18.25-oz) package devil's food cake mix
- ½ (14-oz) can sweetened condensed milk
- 6 oz caramel topping
- 3 bars chocolate-covered toffee, chopped
- 1 (8-oz) container frozen whipped topping, thawed

DIRECTIONS

1. Follow the package directions on the cake mix to make a 9-by-13-inch cake. Cool on a wire rack for 5 to 10 minutes.

2. Using the end of a wooden spoon, poke holes roughly 1 inch apart in a grid across the entire surface of the cake.

3. Combine the condensed milk and caramel in a saucepan over low heat. Stir until smooth and blended. Pour the mixture over the top of the warm cake, letting it sink into the holes, reserving about 2 Tbsp of the mixture for later. Sprinkle the chocolate toffee bars across the top of the warm cake, reserving 2 Tbsp for later. Let cool.

4. Spoon the whipped topping across the top and swirl it into peaks using the back of a spoon. Decorate the top of the cake with the remaining chocolate toffee bar chunks and swirls of the caramel mixture.

5. Refrigerate for at least 2 hours before serving.

MAKES 16 SERVINGS

TIPS AND TRICKS

This recipe uses the poke technique to imbue it with extra flavor and moisture. Other poke cakes can call for chocolate sauce, pudding, or un-set Jell-O.

MIRIAM'S AMISH BUTTER COOKIES

These tender butter cookies are the perfect dessert to serve at the end of a good ol' fashioned Amish lunch or to give as a gift to a parting guest who just won't take the hint he isn't welcome. The best part: No one will be able to tell you didn't wake up at dawn to pound the cream yourself.

INGREDIENTS

- 2 cups butter, softened
- 1½ cups sugar
- 4 egg yolks
- 1½ tsp vanilla extract
- 4½ cups all-purpose flour
- ½ tsp salt

DIRECTIONS

1. Using a hand or stand mixer, cream the butter and sugar in a large bowl. Add in the yolks one at a time, then add in the vanilla.

2. In a separate bowl, whisk together the flour and salt. Stir the dry ingredients into the creamed mixture until a dough forms.

3. Place the ball of dough on a lightly floured surface. Cut in half, then roll each half into a log approximately 2 inches in diameter. Wrap the logs in plastic wrap or wax paper and refrigerate for 4 hours or until firm.

4. Preheat the oven to 350 degrees F.

5. Unwrap the rolls. For added texture, you can roll the logs in chopped nuts or sprinkles before slicing. Slice the logs into ⅜-inch thick rounds. Place the rounds onto ungreased cookie sheets about 2 inches apart.

6. Bake for 8 to 10 minutes. Do not brown.

7. Cool on a wire rack before serving.

MAKES 24 COOKIES

TRIVIA

While the majority of the Amish live in the United States, nearly 5,000 Amish people live in Ontario, the Canadian province where *Schitt's Creek* was filmed.

CITRUS ELEVATION CAKE

If you want a total physical and emotional transformation, allow this upside-down cake to rest for a day before serving to allow the flavors to become elevated and serve with a scoop of vanilla ice cream.

INGREDIENTS

CAKE

- ⅓ cup cornmeal
- ¾ cup buttermilk
- 1¼ cups all-purpose flour
- ½ tsp kosher salt
- 1½ tsp baking powder
- ¼ tsp baking soda
- 1 cup granulated sugar
  Zest of 1 orange
- 1 tsp fresh thyme leaves
- 1 tsp vanilla extract
- ½ cup unsalted butter, room temperature
- 2 large eggs, room temperature

ORANGE LAYER

- ¼ cup unsalted butter
- ¾ cup granulated sugar
- 3 navel oranges, unpeeled, sliced ¼-inch thick

ORANGE GLAZE

- 2 Tbsp fresh-squeezed orange juice
- 1 Tbsp fresh-squeezed lemon juice
- 2 Tbsp granulated sugar

DIRECTIONS

1. In a small bowl, combine the cornmeal and buttermilk. Set the mixture.

2. Preheat the oven to 350 degrees F.

3. Start the orange layer by melting ¼ cup unsalted butter in a microwaveable mug. Pour into the bottom of the 9-inch cake pan. Using a pastry brush, brush the butter up the sides of the pan. Sprinkle ¾ cup sugar over the butter. Push past those demons and layer the orange slices on top of the sugar and butter, starting with one single slice in the center and overlapping the oranges in three concentric, slightly overlapping rings.

4. Place the flour, salt, baking powder, and baking soda in a medium bowl and whisk until the ingredients are well combined, about 30 seconds.

5. Place the sugar in a medium bowl. Add the orange zest and thyme. Use your fingertips to combine until fully incorporated.

6. In the bowl of a stand mixer, add the zested sugar mixture, vanilla, and butter. Beat the butter and sugar mixture on medium speed until light and fluffy, about 3 to 4 minutes, scraping down the sides of the bowl with a rubber spatula as needed.

7. Add one egg at a time, beating after each addition, until combined, then add half of the flour mixture and mix on low speed until incorporated. Add the buttermilk-cornmeal mixture and mix on low speed until combined. Next, add the remaining flour mixture and mix once more on low speed. Scrape

the sides and bottom of the bowl and mix for another 10 seconds. Carefully pour the batter over the orange slices, then smooth the top with a table knife or offset spatula.

8. Bake for 45 minutes or until a toothpick comes out clean. Let cool in the pan for 10 minutes.

9. Meanwhile, combine the orange juice, lemon juice, and sugar in a microwaveable bowl. Microwave the mixture in 30-second increments, stirring after each interval.

Continue until the glaze is about the consistency of honey, 2 to 3 minutes.

10. Run a knife around the edge of the cake pan. Place a plate or platter against the top of the pan and flip it over so that the candied oranges are on top of the cake.

11. Using a pastry brush, brush the cake with the glaze before serving at room temperature.

MAKES 8 SERVINGS

THE CROWS HAVE EYES KIFLE

How best to describe this classic Bosnian breakfast bread?
Well, for starters, it's best eaten post-peregrination from a distant
land, fresh from the oven, served with butter and apricot jam.

INGREDIENTS

- 1⅓ cups warm milk
- ½ cup vegetable oil
- 1 Tbsp active dry yeast
- 2 tsp sugar
- 4 cups all-purpose flour
- 1 tsp salt
- 1 egg white

DIRECTIONS

1. In a medium bowl, combine the milk, oil, yeast, and sugar. Stir gently until the sugar has dissolved. Set aside until bubbles cover the surface, about 5 minutes.

2. In the bowl of a stand mixer, combine the flour and salt, then pour in the yeast mixture. Knead with stand mixer or your hands for about 8 to 10 minutes. The dough should stop sticking to your hands and should be soft, pillowy, and elastic. Cover with a damp kitchen towel and allow to rest in a warm place for 1 to 2 hours or until it has doubled in size.

3. Line two baking sheets with parchment paper. Punch dough down and form it into a ball. Divide it into four even pieces, and then divide each of those pieces into four pieces. Roll each piece into a ball.

4. Flour a work surface. Using a rolling pin, roll one ball into a roughly triangular shape. It should look like a small slice of pizza. Starting from the wide end, roll the dough tightly towards the pointed end until it resembles a croissant. Continue this process with the remaining balls.

5. Place the rolls on the baking sheets. Cover them with a kitchen towel and allow to rise in a warm place for 30 minutes.

6. Preheat the oven to 425 degrees F. Lightly beat the egg white and, when your rolls have risen, brush the tops of each roll.

7. Bake for 12 to 15 minutes until kifle are just golden. Serve warm.

MAKES 16 KIFLE

LOCK AND KEY LIME PIE

Whip up this no-bake pie for your potential match and see if it is the key to their heart! Hopefully, they don't hold it against you that this recipe doesn't have real key limes in it, but it is impossible to get them without driving all the way to Elmdale.

INGREDIENTS

- 1 (3-oz) box of lime Jell-O mix
- 1 (12-oz) can evaporated milk, chilled
- 1 cup sugar
- 2 tsp lime juice
- 2 (8-inch) premade Oreo pie crusts

DIRECTIONS

1. In a small bowl, mix the lime Jell-O and boiling water, stirring until fully dissolved. Refrigerate until the liquid is thick like honey, but not set like Jell-O, about 90 minutes.

2. In a stand mixer, add the chilled evaporated milk and whip until very fluffy. Add the sugar and continue to whip on medium speed for 2 more minutes.

3. Transfer the contents of the stand mixer bowl into another medium bowl. (You do not need to rinse the mixer bowl.) Add the Jell-O liquid and lime juice to the stand mixer bowl and whip on medium until lots of bubbles appear, about 3 minutes. Fold the whipped milk into the Jell-O in two parts, stopping as soon as the color is consistent.

4. Divide the batter into each pie crust.

5. Cover and chill until set, about 4 hours. Serve.

MAKES 12 SERVINGS

TRIVIA

Schitt's Creek only ran for six seasons, but not because it was canceled. The decision to end the show was made by creator Dan Levy, who felt like this chapter of the Rose family's story was told in its entirety over the course of the series.

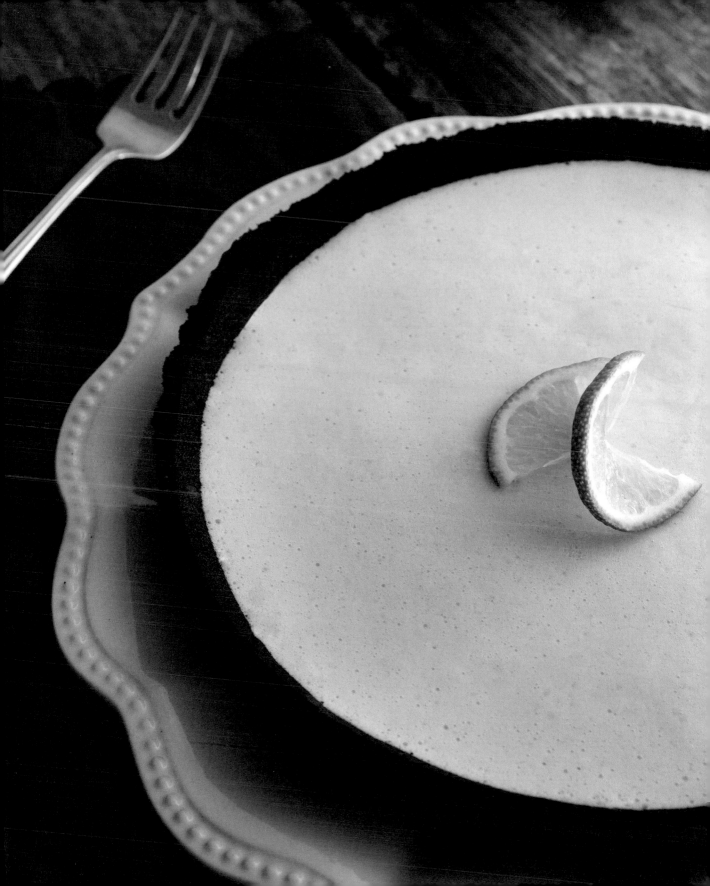

CONVERSION GUIDE

VOLUME

¼ tsp	1 mL
½ tsp	2 mL
1 tsp	5 mL
1 Tbsp	15 mL
¼ cup	50mL
⅓ cup	75 mL
½ cup	125 mL
⅔ cup	150 mL
¾ cup	175 mL
1 cup	250 mL
1 quart	1 liter
1½ quarts	1.5 liters
2 quarts	2 liters
2½ quarts	2.5 liters
3 quarts	3 liters
4 quarts	4 liters

TEMPERATURE

32° F	0° C
212° F	100° C
250° F	120° C
275° F	140° C
300° F	150° C
325° F	160° C
350° F	180° C
375° F	190° C
400° F	200° C
425° F	220° C
450° F	230° C
475° F	240° C
500° F	260° C

LENGTH

⅛ in	3 mm
¼ in	6 mm
½ in	13 mm
¾ in	19 mm
1 in	2.5 cm
2 in	5 cm

WEIGHT

1 oz	30 g
2 oz	55 g
3 oz	85 g
4 oz / ¼ lb	115 g
8 oz / ½ lb	225 g
16 oz / 1 lb	455 g
32 oz / 2 lb	910 g

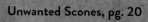
Unwanted Scones, pg. 20

INDEX

ACKNOWLEDGMENTS

TO OUR MOM, Tina, whose frequent and, frankly, uncanny impersonations of Julia Child while cooking nightly dinners inspired us to never take ourselves too seriously in the kitchen. Your lifelong and selfless support of all of our endeavors is a testament to your character as a mother and as a friend. To our recipe testers—Sherril, Brian, Hannah, Kenzie, Dino, Bonnie, and Katie—your feedback, detailed note-taking, and willingness to open your kitchens at the drop of a hat does not go unnoticed or unappreciated. To Phil, our publishing imaginator, who envisaged our pandemic project waggish enough to pursue: Thank you. And, lastly, to our dad, Frank. Thanks to his valiant sacrifice of taste-testing nearly every recipe, we know the dishes in this book are "pretty good" and "even taste like something you'd get from a restaurant."

ABOUT
THE AUTHORS

RACHEL AND HANNAH FLOYD are sisters, native West-Coasters, and huge fans of *Schitt's Creek*. No strangers to cooking, talking, and writing about food, they cut their professional teeth in the culinary industry through years of working behind-the-scenes in restaurants, food blogging, teaching cuisine-related community education classes, and studying recipe development.

Media Lab Books
For inquiries, call 646-449-8614

Published by Topix Media Lab
14 Wall Street, Suite 3C
New York, NY 10005

Printed in China

ISBN-13: 978-1-956403-08-4
ISBN-10: 1-956403-08-6

1C-J23-2